D1320423

Cook-Ahead Cookery

Cook-Ahead Cookery

New, Revised, and Enlarged Edition of
The Working Wives' Cook Book

Theodora Zavin and Fredda Stuart

CROWN PUBLISHERS, INC., NEW YORK

Inquiries should be addressed to Crown Publishers, Inc.,
419 Park Avenue South, New York, N.Y. 10016.

Printed in the United States of America
Published simultaneously in Canada by
General Publishing Company Limited

Library of Congress Cataloging in Publication Data

Zavin, Theodora S
    Cook-ahead cookery.

    First ed. published in 1963 under title: The
working wives' (salaried or otherwise) cook book.
    Includes index.
    1. Cookery.   I.   Stuart, Freda, joint author.
II.   Title.
TX652.Z37   1975   641.5   75–17750
ISBN 0–517–51906–2

*This book is lovingly dedicated to
Benjamin, Jonathan, and Daniel Zavin
and to Fred, Jennifer, and Peter Stuart—
the world's most charming testing
laboratory*

ACKNOWLEDGMENTS

We wish to express our gratitude to those whose interest, ideas, and recipes are such an integral part of this book: Saidie Adwon, Marion Albini, Jane Anton, Gerry Becker, Marion Brown, Miriam Brumer, Pat Burton, Louise Golov, Shirley Greenwald, Rosemarie Haywood, Lillian Itkowitz, Dorris Leggett, Rose Lubin, Winifred Lynn, Chloe Nassau, Ida Null, Patricia Stuart, Emilia Taylor, and Rubin Zavin; and most particularly to Dorothy Freeman, whose recipe file is almost as large as her heart.

Our thanks are due also to Bob Sherwin, who first took our concept of a cookbook seriously; and to Naomi Benowitz for her assistance in the preparation of the manuscript.

Contents

Section One

INTRODUCTION

Back in 1963 the first slender edition of this book was published under the title *The Working Wives' (Salaried or Otherwise) Cook Book*. Time has changed many things. Neither the book nor its authors are quite so slender (though the book has more than doubled in size and we haven't done quite *that* badly) and we've changed the title in recognition of the fact that many of the book's devotees proved to be men, bachelors of both sexes, working mothers without husbands in the house, and a gratifyingly large number of college students. We are, of course, delighted that so many people found the method, approach, and recipes useful and we hope that the change of title will make life easier for those of our readers who felt impelled to keep *The Working Wives' Cook Book* on their shelves in plain brown wrapper.

While we cherish all our readers, much of this introduction is still directed to the working wife because there still seems to be no other book aimed at the particular life-style of the working woman who cooks for a family. If you don't happen to be a working wife, come along and eavesdrop anyway. Whatever your reason for being unwilling or unable to spend the afternoon preparing dinner, we think you'll find some interesting ideas on how to prepare a stew without getting into one.

It is, of course, possible for a working wife to feed her family on frozen convenience foods, broiled meats, Kentucky

1

Fried Chicken, and an occasional trip to McDonald's as a gustatory highlight. You can get away with it if your mother-in-law was a terrible cook and you carefully shield your children from contact with real home-cooked meals. Some people do. (One of our sons found that one of the more startling experiences of his military career was the discovery that there were men who thought army food was good!) But the rewards of feeding your family well far outweigh the time and trouble. Vanity alone should be some motivation. We have never known a man who waxed nostalgic over his mother's ability to shine floors or a child who liked to bring his friends home to enjoy his mother's prowess in getting stubborn stains out of dungarees. But, a lovely pedestal awaits the woman who cooks!

Vanity aside, we do really do believe that today when so many elements are conspiring to pull the family structure apart, family dinner represents a rare and precious opportunity for warmth and fun and communication—provided that it isn't made into a harried, tense, unpleasant interval by a harried, tense, unpleasant cook.

A number of cookbooks have tried to eliminate time as the *sine qua non* of good cooking, and it might seem as if these "quick" cookbooks were the answer to the problems of the working wife. What then—besides a fearful compulsion for recipe swapping—made us decide to add another cookbook to the shelves?

We find the usual run of "quick" cookbooks inadequate for several reasons. Some of them lean heavily on garnishing prepared foods. To us, a quarter-cup of burgundy added to a can of beef stew tastes quite like a can of beef stew with a quarter-cup of burgundy added to it. Many of the recipes seem to revolve around canned cream of mushroom soup, to which you add meat, fish, or chicken. These dishes are quick and economical and they lend a certain harmony to your cooking. Everything tastes like cream of mushroom soup.

Most important, however, is the fact that most of the really good "quick" cookbooks enable the cook to get dinner on the table within one to one-and-a-half hours after her arrival home, provided that she dashes madly from the front door to the kitchen without removing her hat and juggles pots, chops onions, and generally goes frantic for an hour or so before dinner is ready. This procedure has a few obvious drawbacks.

While we are second to none in our admiration of the working wife, it must be admitted that she lacks some of the fine lasting qualities of an electronic computer. After a long day's work, no respectable IBM machine feels a desire to take off its shoes or have a drink.

This is a tough hour of the day in which to scramble. It is just at this time that children (and husbands, too!) want and deserve attention. It's hard to listen to the story of today's basketball game, prescribe for a wounded doll, and measure out ingredients simultaneously. What's the alternative—other than hiring a cook or spending precious weekend time cooking and freezing for the week ahead? The solution lies in preparing most of each day's dinner the night before. And there's the essence of our system.

We know several things about the working wife. She is not a habitué of Maxwell's Plum. She spends many, if not most, weekday evenings at home. She gets her second wind after the children are in bed, and that's the magic time to do the few things in the kitchen that will enable her to spend most of her post-homecoming hour with a child on her lap or a drink in her hand (both, if she's a talented type), with only an occasional foray into the kitchen to pop things into the oven or onto the dinner table.

Although this book was planned primarily by and for working wives, we think it has great value for what are (laughingly, we hope) known as "nonworking" wives—those "ladies of leisure" with three preschool children, eighteen committees, and questions like "Honey, do you mind if I bring Bob Kirk of our Atlanta office home for dinner one night this week?" The cook-ahead dinner makes for lovely entertaining because Frazzled Hostess is not served as the first course.

We think that this method of cooking will prove valuable also to any mother of a small baby or a toddler. Even the best of babies tend to get fractious toward the end of the day. At their cheeriest, they still need to be bathed, fed, and made ready for bed. All of this is a little difficult to do with patience and good humor, much less enjoyment, if the bulk of the preparation for the family dinner must also be done at this time. If the work for dinner has been done either the night before or while the baby was taking a morning nap, the end of the day can become a pleasant, relaxed time for both mother and baby rather than a nightmare which leaves a tired, tight-lipped wife to greet her husband.

The trick is to sit down on Friday evening with the next week's engagement calendar at hand and two sheets of paper— one to make up the week's menus in light of how much time is available each evening, and the other for the week's shopping that you do on Saturday. This will take about half an hour, and it's a shrewd investment of your time. For one thing, you'll no longer be seized by the "what'll we have for dinner tonight" panic that grips you as you lock your desk. For another, you'll no longer have to make a daily trip to the supermarket or leave shopping lists for your grumbling children. Planning your menus for a week at a time is also a great boon to the budget. It enables you to balance off a meal with fairly expensive ingredients with one less costly. It also helps to avoid getting stuck with limp leftovers. If you're planning a dish that's going to require you to buy a bunch of celery to get one stalk, that's a fine week to plan on making the vegetable soup on page 222 that will effectively use up more of the celery.

This is a collection of recipes that lend themselves beautifully to being prepared, and, in some cases, partially or fully cooked the night before. Some of them are one-dish meals and need no addition other than salad, bread, and dessert. Others

4

could use a vegetable or two served on the side. While we have included recipes for some appetizers, soups, salads, vegetables, and desserts, we have concentrated primarily on main courses. If your main dish is good, you can use canned or frozen vegetables with or without one of the flourishes suggested on pages 206–8; nothing more elaborate is needed. No one but a gourmet society demands that every course be terribly special.

Although we haven't a kind word to say about the frozen dinners in your market's freezer, we have great enthusiasm for *your* frozen dinners (or parts thereof) in *your* freezer. When you're making a dish that can be doubled with very little additional time or effort, you can make two meals for the price —in time and effort, at least—of one. For example, if you double the pot roast recipe on page 28, your additional preparation time, including slicing the meat for freezing, probably won't exceed 10 to 15 minutes. And that's an extra meal tucked away for a night when you haven't time or just don't feel like cooking.

Some of the recipes in this book require a minimum of night-before time in the kitchen. They are fine for the night of a PTA meeting or a bridge foursome. Others, which require longer cooking, are better for the evenings when nothing special is on the program and the cook can go into the kitchen to stir or add an ingredient during the TV commercial, at the end of a chapter, or while she's getting the coffee for the friends who dropped in.

You will notice that each recipe indicates both the preparation time and the cooking time involved both the night before and just before serving. Obviously, the preparation time will vary a little from cook to cook, depending on the arrangement of the kitchen and the tempo at which you work. Our preparation times are based on the assumption that you will be using efficient equipment. If, for example, you beat egg whites by hand instead of using an electric mixer, your preparation time will run somewhat longer than indicated. We use an electric skillet for browning large quantities of meat or fowl. If you do this in a nonelectric pan, you will find that you cannot brown as much at one time and that you must stay in the kitchen to move the pieces around to get even browning. This, too, will increase the preparation time.

We use the words "preparation time" to mean all the time you must spend in the kitchen. For the most part, this comes before the cooking process. Where, however, you must return to the kitchen during or at the end of the cooking time to stir or add ingredients, that time is also included in computing the preparation time.

You will notice that the ingredients for some of the recipes are separated into two groups by a dotted line. The ingredients listed above the dotted line are those you will need in your night-before preparation; the ones below the dotted line are those that will be added on the night you are serving the dish.

A word about the size of our recipes. With some exceptions, they are designed to serve four—not four dainty home economists who try them out in their laboratory kitchens at lunchtime, but a family of four real people. Nothing frustrates us quite so much as following a recipe supposedly adequate for four, only to find that it's barely enough for one adolescent son. It frustrates the adolescent son, too. This is most undesirable because, as you will see in the next section, we have other plans for him!

THE WHEREWITHAL

*A Guide to the Effective Use of
Electric Power, Spouse Power, and Child Power*

When the first edition of this book was published, one reviewer noted rather crossly that we seemed to lean rather heavily on the use of electric appliances. It is a measure of how times have changed that we felt it necessary in 1963 to spend more than three pages on an impassioned plea that the working wife really needed a dishwasher! This is an argument that need hardly be made today. Similarly, few people who cook constantly would consider the electric mixer, blender, and skillet unnecessary frills.

One thing, however, hasn't changed. We are still passionate devotees of the electric appliances that save woman-power and, since we have a whole new list of them, the cross reviewer may just as well start sharpening her pencil again.

For a lady of infinite leisure, some of the appliances that we consider worth their weight in truffles might be merely nice to have. For the woman who works, they represent a means of freeing her to play Parcheesi, pat-a-cake, or bridge (London or Goren), depending on the ages and the interests of her family.

High on our list of worthwhile equipment is the electric meat grinder. Aside from the fact that there are some dishes which can't as a practical matter be made without one, it is the kind of gadget one uses for more purposes than expected— from grinding up the tail of a steak to preparing baby food. Someday, if our trusty blender, mixer, and grinder all go to that great kitchen in the sky simultaneously, we're going to try out an appliance called a "Cuisinart Food Processor," which the redoubtable James Beard characterizes as "like having another person in the kitchen." It performs the function of all three appliances and mixes pastry or biscuit dough as well. If you're starting from scratch or have a rich aunt pining to spend about $175 on a present for you, this is an appliance you might want to look at.

At the other end of the scale, here's an appliance that currently costs about $12 and is guaranteed to repay its cost in time and money in the first month. It's called a Dazey Seal-A-Meal and hangs on your kitchen wall ready to seal food in special plastic bags for freezing. These plastic bags of food, like the ones of creamed vegetables sold at the market, are heated by dropping into boiling water. Unlike the ones you get at the market, however, the food in them is economical, to your taste since you cooked it, and in the right amounts for your use because you have your choice of three sizes of bags in which you can freeze small or large quantities. An additional advantage is that you can put your food along with an appropriate amount of gravy or sauce all in the bag without fear that it will dry out when reheated. And no pot to wash! This is an unadvertised and relatively little known appliance, but to know it is to love it. One of us recently hosted a bridal shower and gave the bride-to-be a Seal-A-Meal as a gift. Since nobody other than the giver knew what the gadget was for, the whole party moved into the kitchen for a demonstration. Within a month, more than three-quarters of the guests had acquired one of their own.

One of us is an avid Chinese cook and a fan of the electric wok. Purists argue that it doesn't change temperature as quickly as the top-of-the-stove kind, but it does so well enough for home use and has the additional advantage of being easy to clean, attractive enough to take to the table, and capable of keeping food warm if you can't serve the second your dish is ready. It also doubles beautifully as a deep-fryer, thereby saving another gadget, and, with the use of a pie plate to hold a dish of food, it can be used as a steamer as well.

A large electric warming tray, or, better still, a tea cart whose entire top is a heating unit, is another cook-saver. You can put the whole dinner on at once, hot dishes on the top shelf and cold ones below, and serve firsts, seconds, and thirds without moving from your chair. It may also save you from a charge of aggravated assault if yours is the kind of family that doesn't get around to washing up until dinner is cooling on the table. It will hold food at the heat you want without further cooking for an astonishingly long period with no loss of flavor or texture.

We think that you will find this cookbook useful even if you don't at the moment have any or all of the appliances we love so dearly. But if you really want to use a night-before cooking system, we strongly recommend that you accumulate a set of casseroles that can go directly from the refrigerator into the oven or vice versa and that can also be used for top-of-the-stove cooking. Most glass casseroles can't take this kind of change of temperature without being given a chance to warm up or cool down to room temperature first; furthermore, not all casseroles can be used over a burner. There are now available, however, casseroles of several kinds that can do all these things. The lovely Dansk casseroles, which are enamel over metal, can. The Corning Ware casseroles can, too. There are others, but careful shopping is in order here.

Your casseroles should also have the further virtue of being sufficiently good-looking to go straight to the table. This not only saves you time in getting dinner on but obviously cuts down on the dishwashing problem as well.

The most useful kitchen aid of all, of course, is an extra pair of hands attached to a willing body—otherwise known as a helpful husband. How much help a working wife has from this source depends, we suspect, on the age and environment of the couple. Back in 1959, Dr. Shirley Greenwald wrote a fascinating dissertation analyzing the housekeeping patterns of a group of forty-four working wives and mothers.* In only a minute fraction of the families did the husband participate in any of the housekeeping chores. It would be interesting to know, fifteen years and one women's liberation movement later, how much that pattern has changed. Unfortunately, we know of no recent similar study. We suspect, however, that the greatest change has come about among younger couples and that it is probably most discernible among the well-educated, where the most serious reappraisal of roles has taken place in the last decade. It also seems to us that, as the fixed line between what is considered "womanly" and "manly" has begun to waver, more men feel free to enjoy the fun and creativity of cooking. Fewer men, nowadays, work in jobs where you can see the result of your day's labor in terms of a plowed field or a finished table. Perhaps this is why an increasing number of men find cooking so satisfying to the soul; it produces something which can be seen, touched and enjoyed in immediate, tangible form.

If you're lucky enough to have a husband whose share of the household chores includes part of the preparation for dinner or cleaning up afterward, you're way ahead of the game. But don't overlook a labor-saving device that you may already have and that will cost you nothing extra to operate effectively: CHILDREN! Aside from any other chores you may be able to coax out of them by reciting the Fifth Commandment in meaningful tones, the objective toward which the working mother should strive is that one child has the job of setting the table for dinner and another the responsibility of clearing it after the main course, and serving dessert and beverage. If you have a third child, he can load the dishwasher; otherwise that job has to be distributed among the available ones. In the absence of a dish-

* Greenwald, *Family Responsibilities of Working Mothers* (New York: School of Education, New York University, 1959).

washer, it will usually take all the available children (unless you're blessed with a very large family) to do the dishes. The objective is that Mama should not have to set foot in the kitchen from the time she serves the main course until she goes back some hours later to prepare the next night's dinner. Sharing the responsibility is not only good for the children's souls but also makes for a rested and relaxed mother who can enjoy her evening hours with her family. What you need in order to reach this goal is to start the children working early in life so that they do their share without questioning it (until they reach adolescence, at which point they will question whatever you do, think, or look like anyway). This takes a certain amount of strength of character. You have to force yourself to sit quietly at the table while the children clear by taking one dish at a time or trying twelve, while they argue about whose turn it is to do what and generally tempt you to declare that it would be easier to do it yourself. It would, but you're not building for the future that way.

RANDOM THOUGHTS
AND
(WE HOPE) HELPFUL HINTS

The proper utensil for chopping canned tomatoes is a potato masher; the proper way to mash potatoes, however, is with an electric mixer.

. . . .

Many recipes call for fresh gingerroot, which can be bought in oriental, Spanish, and Mexican food stores, among others, or by mail from one of the sources listed on page 12. Ginger can be kept indefinitely in your refrigerator if you peel it, put it in a small jar, pour enough sherry into the jar to cover the ginger, and cover the jar tightly.

. . . .

Many electric stoves have a very low heat setting that makes double boilers unnecessary. If you haven't one of those, your hardware store probably has a metal plate (a popular one is called a Flametainer) that goes over the flame and shields your pot from direct heat.

. . . .

If you have *two* sets of measuring spoons hung on your wall, you'll save yourself years of the irritation of having to wash and dry a tablespoon you've just used for oil, before you can dip it in the sugar bowl.

. . . .

Two hints on making pastry: The dough is easier to handle if you refrigerate it for an hour before rolling. Secondly, never roll your rolling pin from one end of the dough to the other; always start it in the middle and roll out to the edge, turning the dough frequently until it becomes too large to turn easily.

. . . .

We've never been able to understand why people who will tackle French cooking with aplomb are intimidated by Chinese cooking. It really isn't difficult and it has the advantages of low cost, low calories, low cholesterol, and great taste. It's particularly suitable for the working wife because ingredients can be chopped or mixed in advance and cooked very quickly. We've given you just a few Chinese recipes to get you started. If you can't find the occasional Chinese ingredients in a local store, you can order by mail from one of the following, all of whom will send you a catalogue on request:

Four Seas International, P.O. Box 22, Williston Park, N.Y. 11596, or 345 Pennsylvania Avenue, Mineola, N.Y. 11501.
Kam Shing Co., 2246 South Wentworth Avenue, Chicago, Ill. 60616. (Enclose 10-cent stamp for catalogue.)
Kwong On Lung Importers, 680 North Spring Street, Los Angeles, Calif. 90012.

Oyama's Oriental Food Shop, 1302 Amsterdam Avenue, New York, N.Y. 10027.

. . . .

For years we tried to skewer poultry cavities, baked fish, and similar dishes and ended up with skewer-scarred hands and stuffing all over the baking pan. Rescue came in the form of a trussing needle—a very large, sharp needle with a large eye that will sew meat or fish together in a whisk using butcher cord, which can easily be seen and removed after cooking so that your guests don't end up with a mouthful of thread. Usually available at gourmet cookware shops for under 50 cents, it will save its cost in Band-Aids.

. . . .

We confess that our recommendations of dishes for freezing are somewhat subjective. Actually you can freeze practically anything other than broiled or sautéed foods, cooked potatoes, raw salad vegetables, and dishes with a lot of mayonnaise. It's also advisable not to freeze a dish whose ingredients have previously been frozen. We've suggested the possibility of freezing only for those dishes that either take little additional time to double or give us that oh-what-the-hell-as-long-as-I'm-at-it feeling. If you've got your floured bread board and rolling pin out anyway, it seems like a good idea to roll a second batch of Cornish Pastries. It's also useful if you're planning a party and want to cut down on the amount you have to do the night before the festivities.

We purposely haven't indicated in most cases the cooking time for frozen food. This is because it will vary depending on how cold your freezer is. The freezer compartment of a refrigerator may be zero and a full freezer may be 25° below. For the latter, cooking time may be double the time indicated for refrigerated food while it may be only fifty percent more if your freezer isn't too cold. If the frozen food is allowed to thaw in the refrigerator before being cooked, the cooking time is the same as that for unfrozen food. Foods frozen in the Seal-A-

Meal bags are never defrosted before cooking and take between 15 and 25 minutes in boiling water, depending on the density of the package.

Cream soups or gravies may appear to separate in freezing but can be stirred together again. Place the freezing container in a pot of hot water halfway up the sides of the container until the block loosens enough to be tipped into a pot. Stir frequently while reheating.

. . . .

There comes a time in the life of every cook, no matter how forehanded she may be, when steaks, chops, and London broil become the order of the day—either because she has absolutely no time the night before or because her family likes them. Formulas for cooking a steak are almost as legion as recipes for "the only decent way" to mix a Martini. We think ours is the second-best way—nothing, of course, can compete with charcoal broiling. The secret is soy sauce, which gives you the kind of crisp outside crust ordinarily obtainable only by charcoal grilling.

Here's the plot: if you have a spare 15 minutes before dinner, pour some soy sauce into a large platter or shallow roasting pan (not aluminum, please) and marinate the steaks or chops for 15 minutes, turning the meat occasionally. (If you crush a clove of garlic into the soy sauce, it won't do a bit of harm.) If you're short on time, just brush the soy sauce on both sides of the meat, using a pastry brush. Cook in an uncovered, ungreased skillet (375° if you're using an electric pan) until done. You can broil the meat if you prefer. We like the skillet because it's easier to clean and produces results that are just as good as the broiler.

It's a little difficult to give exact times for these dishes because the time will vary with the thickness of the meat and the exact point on the spectrum from rare to well done your family prefers for its meat. The following are suggested as a rough guide; test the meat by making a small cut in the center to see if it's done to your taste:

Steak: 4 to 5 minutes on each side will give you a rare steak if it's about 1 inch thick.

Lamb chops: 9 minutes on each side.

Veal chops: 10 to 11 minutes on each side.

London broil: 4 minutes on each side (medium rare). Score the meat lightly on each side before marinating or brushing with the soy sauce. With the London broil, try a can of mushroom gravy to which you have added ½ teaspoon minced garlic. Slice the meat by cutting at about a 45° angle.

Soy sauce also does lovely things to broiled chicken. Brush it over the chicken before broiling and don't add any other seasoning. Try brushing it over hamburgers, too.

Soy sauce can, incidentally, be used over again if you strain and refrigerate it between uses.

. . . .

Minced dried garlic is a substitute for fresh garlic if you're short of time or just lazy. There is another garlic trick, however, which is less well known. Take a few unpeeled garlic cloves and plant them in a little flowerpot, with the blunt edge of the clove down and the pointed edge just barely covered with earth. Put the pot on your kitchen windowsill and water it when you think of it. In a week or so you will see green shoots sprouting from your garlic cloves. When they are about 6 inches tall, start using them. When you need garlic, simply take your kitchen shears and snip off as much as you want and toss it into the pot. The shoots will keep growing after cutting, and a single planting should last you for a few months. These pretty green shoots have no odor, but if you have any doubt that they have an authentic garlic flavor, just cut off a bit and taste it. This is a lovely way to use garlic because you get no garlic smell on your hands and you are relieved of the problems of peeling and chopping the cloves.

. . . .

A kitchen timer will save you time and mental effort. Let the timer remember to tell you when a dish is ready or when you have to go back into the kitchen to add ingredients.

.   .   .   .

When broiling shish kebab, you can make them much easier to turn by placing the skewers over a shallow baking dish. Leave the last half inch of each skewer unfilled; then suspend the skewers across the top of the baking dish. This method also makes it easier to baste the shish kebab and to collect sauce to pour over them before serving. For those who loathe cleaning broilers and broiler trays, there's a bonus; you just need to wash the baking dish—a much easier job.

.   .   .   .

Kitchen scissors or shears are sometimes much easier to use than a knife—for chopping scallion tops, dicing bacon, snipping parsley or dill, or cutting green beans.

.   .   .   .

One of the assets of cooking the night before is that it is possible to get rid of fat you'd never know was there if your cooking was done in one continuous process. After overnight refrigeration, the chilled fat can easily be skimmed off the surface.

Section Two

MAIN DISHES

□ BEEF □

Madeira Sauce for Steak or Roast Beef

1 tablespoon butter
6 large fresh mushrooms, sliced
2 tablespoons minced shallots
¼ teaspoon salt

¼ teaspoon pepper
½ cup Madeira wine
1 can (10¾ oz.) beef gravy

The Night Before

Preparation Time: 10 min.   *Cooking Time:* 15 min.

Melt butter over medium heat, add sliced mushrooms and sauté for 5 minutes.

Add shallots and cook until most of the liquid in the pan has evaporated.

Add Madeira and cook over high heat for 1 minute. Lower heat to medium, add gravy, salt, and pepper, and cook 15 minutes.

Cover and refrigerate.

Before Serving

Preparation Time: 1 min.   *Cooking Time:* 10 min.

Cook on top of stove until heated through.   *2 cups*

Basic Meat Sauce

This started out as a spaghetti sauce. Because it is almost as easy to make a large quantity as a small one, our practice has been to make it on a rainy Sunday and freeze most of it for future use. Over the years we've found that we tend to use a good part of our supply for purposes other than a spaghetti sauce—for the cannelloni on page 152, the lasagna on page 164. Not bad as a filling for tacos, either.

½ lb. bacon
2½ lbs. chopped chuck
2 cups chopped onion
2 green peppers, washed and seeded
2 cloves garlic
3 cans Italian plum tomatoes (2 lb. 3 oz. size)

3 (6-ounce) cans tomato paste
¾ cup chopped parsley
1½ cups dry red wine
3 tablespoons salt
1 teaspoon pepper
3 tablespoons oregano
2 tablespoons basil

The Night Before

Preparation Time: 40 min.   *Cooking Time:* 3 hrs.

Cut bacon in ½ inch pieces and fry until crisp in a very large saucepan or Dutch oven.

While the bacon is frying, chop the onion. Chop the green peppers and garlic.

When the bacon is crisp, remove it from the pan and set aside to drain on a paper towel. Discard all but 2 tablespoons of the bacon fat. Add the meat and cook, stirring frequently, until it is browned.

Add the garlic, onion, and green pepper to the meat and cook for 10 minutes, stirring occasionally. While it is cooking, chop the parsley and open the cans of tomatoes and tomato paste. Discard the liquid from two of the cans of tomatoes.

Add the tomatoes, mashing with the side of a metal spoon or with a potato masher; add all the remaining ingredients.

Bring to a boil, lower heat, and simmer, uncovered, for 3 hours, stirring occasionally.

Cool before refrigerating or freezing.

Before Serving

The time it takes to reheat the sauce will, of course, depend on whether it has been refrigerated or frozen.

4 Quarts
Can be frozen

Beef Stroganoff

3 tablespoons butter	5 teaspoons prepared mustard
3 tablespoons flour	2 large onions
2 cups beef broth, boiling	¼ lb. fresh mushrooms

. . . .

1½ lbs. sirloin, cut in ¼-inch strips (see note on page 24)	3 tablespoons butter 6 tablespoons sour cream

The Night Before

Preparation and Cooking Time: 10 min.

Melt butter in a saucepan. Add flour and blend. Add the broth all at one time. Stir and cook until thick. Stir in mustard. Cover and refrigerate sauce.

Slice onions and mushrooms and refrigerate in a plastic bag.

Before Serving

Preparation and Cooking Time: 15 min.

Melt butter in a large skillet (350° if using an electric pan) and sauté onions and mushrooms briefly just until they are soft.

Add beef strips and cook briefly until meat is browned on both sides.

While the beef is cooking, reheat the sauce. Add the sour cream and stir until hot but not boiling.

Pour the sauce over the beef mixture in the skillet and serve.

Serves 4
Can be frozen

Steak with Wine Sauce

If you're feeling extravagant, this dish is best made with filet mignon. It can, however, be made with boneless sirloin. In either case, the steak should be about 1 inch thick and about ½ lb. per serving.

1 cup chicken broth	2 teaspoons Bovril beef extract
1 cup red wine	2 tablespoons minced parsley
½ cup onion, chopped	1 tablespoon red wine vinegar
¼ cup dill pickle, chopped	1 teaspoon salt
6 tablespoons butter	¼ teaspoon pepper
12 large mushrooms	

. . . .

2 lbs. steak, cut in 4 portions (see note above)	4 slices trimmed white bread (or French bread cut on a slant)

The Night Before

Preparation Time: 15 min. *Cooking Time:* 45 min.

Place broth, wine, chopped onion, and pickle in saucepan. Bring to a boil, reduce heat, and cook over moderate flame until liquid is reduced to about 1 cup—this will take about ½ hour.

While sauce is simmering, melt 3 tablespoons of butter in a wide pan. Add the mushrooms and sauté gently, covered, for about 5 minutes, turning once. Refrigerate mushrooms in pan in which they were cooked.

When the liquid in the wine mixture is reduced, add the remaining 3 tablespoons of butter and stir until melted. Remove from flame, add beef extract, parsley, vinegar, salt, and pepper. Let it cool slightly, then put it in a blender and blend at high speed for 1 minute. Cover and refrigerate.

Before Serving

Preparation and Cooking Time: 10 min.

Reheat mushrooms in pan in which they were cooked. Reheat sauce.

Cook steaks in an ungreased pan for 3 to 4 minutes per side depending on the degree of rareness you want.

Toast bread.

To serve, place each steak on a slice of toast, top with 3 mushrooms, and pour some of the sauce over the top. Pass the rest of the sauce in a gravy boat.   *Serves 4*

Deviled Short Ribs

3 lbs. beef short ribs, cut in
    4 pieces
1 quart water
¼ cup cider vinegar
1 tablespoon salt
¼ teaspoon pepper
¾ cup ketchup
¾ cup prepared mustard

¾ cup corn syrup
3 tablespoons horseradish,
    drained
2 cloves garlic, minced
1 tablespoon Worcestershire
    sauce
1 teaspoon Tabasco

The Night Before

Preparation Time: 12 min.   *Cooking Time:* 1½ hrs.

Put the meat into a large pot together with the water, vinegar, salt, and pepper. Bring to a boil, reduce heat and simmer, covered, for 1½ hours. Drain and discard liquid.

Mix all remaining ingredients together in a bowl.

Place meat in a roasting pan and pour the sauce over it. Cover and refrigerate. The next morning turn the meat and baste the other side with the sauce before re-covering and refrigerating.

Before Serving

Preparation Time: 7 min.   *Cooking Time:* 25 min.

Heat oven to 425°.

Bake, uncovered, for 25 minutes, turning and basting the meat 3 or 4 times during the cooking period.   *Serves 4*
            Can be frozen

Tamale Pie

4 cups water
1 teaspoon salt
5 chicken bouillon cubes (or powder)
1 cup cornmeal
1 lb. ground chuck
1 small onion, chopped
1 small green pepper, seeded and chopped
2 cloves garlic, minced

1 can (1-lb.) tomatoes in puree
1 package (10-oz.) frozen corn
1 tablespoon (or more) chili powder
¼ cup sliced black olives
¼ cup sliced green olives stuffed with pimiento
1 cup grated cheddar cheese

The Night Before
Preparation and Cooking Time: 25 min.

Add salt to water and bring to boil in a large saucepan. Slowly add cornmeal and stir until mixture returns to boil. Turn heat very low, cover, and cook 15 minutes or until mixture thickens. Stir occasionally.

Meanwhile, chop onion and green pepper and mince garlic. Slowly brown ground beef, onion, garlic, and green pepper in frying pan. (No fat is necessary unless you have unusually lean ground beef.)

When the meat has browned, add tomatoes, corn, and chili powder. Cook for 10 to 15 minutes. Add olives.

After the cornmeal mixture has cooked and cooled slightly, grease a 2-quart casserole and line it with most of the cornmeal as if you were forming a pie shell. Reserve about 1½ cups of cornmeal.

Pour meat-corn-tomato mixture in. Spoon reserved cornmeal around outer edge on top of meat. Sprinkle grated cheddar cheese in center. Cover and refrigerate.

Before Serving
Preparation Time: 1 min.   *Cooking Time:* 1½ hrs.

Preheat oven to 350°. Remove casserole from refrigerator and uncover.

Bake for 1½ hours.   *Serves 6 to 8*

Beef Scallops

8 slices cut from beef round, ⅛″ thick
3 slices white bread
2 tablespoons grated Parmesan cheese
½ teaspoon salt

¼ teaspoon pepper
½ cup flour
1 egg
½ lb. fresh mushrooms
2 tablespoons butter

. . . .

2 tablespoons butter
1 tablespoon olive oil

½ cup dry red wine

The Night Before

Preparation Time: 25 to 30 min.   *Cooking Time:* 10 min.

If the butcher has not done it for you, cut eight very thin slices from the top or bottom round of beef. (Partial freezing makes it easier to cut thin slices.)

Make fresh bread crumbs by tearing bread and running a few pieces at a time through the blender. Add Parmesan cheese, salt, and pepper to bread crumbs and place on a dish. Put flour and lightly beaten egg on separate dishes.

Dip each piece of beef first in flour, then in egg, then in bread crumb mixture. Place on platter, cover, and refrigerate.

Slice mushrooms. Melt butter in frying pan and sauté mushrooms over medium-high heat for about 10 minutes. Cover and refrigerate in the pan in which they were cooked.

Before Serving

Preparation and Cooking Time: 10 min.

Reheat mushrooms. Meanwhile heat butter and oil together in a large skillet, add beef slices, and cook quickly until brown on both sides—it should take 4 or 5 minutes altogether.

Remove meat and keep warm on serving platter. Add wine to pan in which beef was cooked, and cook and stir over high heat for a minute or two. Add mushrooms, cook for a minute or two longer. Pour sauce over meat and serve sauce separately in a gravy boat.   *Serves 4*

Chinese Beef and Peppers

This recipe is offered with a slight apology because, unlike most in this book, it may require you to have your pre-dinner drink in the kitchen. The preparation time immediately before dinner takes only 20 min., but that time involves a fair amount of adding ingredients and stirring. Our apology is, however, slight, since this dish has the virtue of being almost irresistible to the male animals of our acquaintance.

While we've never fed this dish to our respective butchers, they are among the male animals whom we cultivate assiduously. A cook's greatest asset is a friendly butcher who feels slightly protective about her. If you have that kind, he'll cheerfully slice the sirloin for you. Otherwise, put it in the freezing compartment for an hour before slicing it.

1½ lbs. sirloin, 1 inch thick, sliced in ⅛-inch slivers
4 green peppers, sliced in thin rings

3 medium onions, sliced
5 scallions (green onions) with green tops, sliced
3 to 4 cups boiling water

· · · · · · · · · · · ·

3 tablespoons salad oil
1 teaspoon salt
2 cloves of garlic, chopped
2 teaspoons Accent (monosodium glutamate)
1½ teaspoons sugar

⅛ teaspoon pepper
¾ cup beef bouillon
3 tablespoons cornstarch
2 tablespoons soy sauce
¾ cup cold water

The Night Before

Preparation Time: 15 to 20 min.

Slice the sirloin if the butcher has not already done so and return it to refrigerator.

Pour enough boiling water over pepper rings to cover completely. Let stand 5 min., rinse in cold water. Meanwhile, slice the onions and scallions. Store the onions, scallions and peppers all together in the refrigerator in a covered dish or plastic bag.

Before Serving

Preparation Time: 20 min. *Cooking Time:* 25 min.
(including preparation time)

Heat oil in a large skillet or wok. Add the peppers, onions, scallions, salt, and garlic. Cook, stirring, over high heat (375° if you're using an electric skillet) for about 3 min. Add beef and cook, stirring, for 3 min. more. Add Accent, sugar, and pepper and cook for 1 more min. Add the boullion and bring to the boiling point.

While this is cooking, put ¾ cup cold water in a measuring cup and add the cornstarch and soy sauce to it. Mix well, then stir it into the skillet mixture. Stir and cook until the sauce is thickened and translucent—about 4 min.   *Serves 4*

Cheese Stuffed Meatloaf

This dish has two practical considerations to recommend it. It's fast to make and it's an excellent budget balancer for a week when you want an inexpensive main dish to set off a slightly extravagant one. Neither of these would be convincing reasons for making it, however, if it weren't a tasty dish. It is.

1½ lbs. chopped chuck	1 green pepper, chopped
6 tablespoons barbecue sauce	½ cup chopped onion
1 teaspoon garlic salt	¾ cup shredded Cheddar cheese

The Night Before
Preparation Time: 10 min.

Mix the beef, barbecue sauce, and garlic salt together. Put half on the bottom of a 1-quart casserole.

Chop the onion and green pepper and sprinkle them together with the cheese on top of the layer of meat. Cover with the remainder of the meat mixture.

Before Serving
Preparation Time: 1 min.   *Cooking Time:* 40 min.

Remove casserole from refrigerator and heat oven to 350°.

Bake, uncovered, for 40 minutes.

Serves 4

Steak Diane

This is a fine main course for a meal when you have practically no time the night before or when you prefer to spend your available time making a very special soup, dessert, or what-have-you.

Serving this dish produces a very interesting phenomenon: it guarantees a rush to the kitchen after dinner so that somebody gets to mop up any stray sauce left in the pan with rye or Italian bread or whatever happens to be available.

The cooking time will vary a little depending on whether you have a skillet large enough to handle all the steak at once or whether you have to do it in two batches.

3 scallions (including green),
    diced

    . . . .

4 tablespoon butter

2½ lbs. boneless sirloin, sliced
    ¼ inch thick

3 tablespoons freeze-dried or
    bottled chives

3 tablespoons parsley flakes

3 tablespoons Worcestershire
    sauce

3 tablespoons A-1 sauce

¼ cup cognac (optional)

The Night Before

Preparation Time: 3 min.

Wash and chop scallions. Refrigerate in a plastic bag or covered dish.

Before Serving

Preparation and Cooking Time: 10 to 15 min.

Heat large skillet over medium flame or heat electric frying pan to 350°. Melt 2 tablespoons of the butter, add the scallions and cook for 1 minute, stirring.

Add steaks and cook briefly on both sides. When the steaks are done, put them into a pan with a tightly fitting lid.

Add remaining butter to pan of scallions along with the chives, parsley, Worcestershire, and A-1. Mix. Add any juices from the pan in which the steak is waiting and mix again.

Replace steaks in skillet and reheat briefly, turning so both sides get covered with sauce.

If you wish to add the cognac, warm it briefly in a separate pan, ignite, and pour the sauce over the steaks.   *Serves 4*

Chili con Carne

2 tablespoons vegetable
   or olive oil
1 onion, chopped
1 clove garlic, minced
1 lb. ground chuck
6 tablespoons tomato paste
1 to 1½ cups water

1 to 2 tablespoons chili powder
1 teaspoon salt
½ teaspoon cumin
¼ teaspoon crushed red pepper
   (optional)
1 can red kidney beans

The Night Before

Preparation Time: 8 min.   *Cooking Time:* 30 min.

Heat oil in large saucepan. Chop onion, mince garlic, and add both to oil. Cook for about 5 minutes or until the onion is soft and translucent. Add ground chuck and cook until meat is no longer red.

Add tomato paste and stir. Add 1 cup water, stir, cook over fairly high heat for a minute or two. If the sauce seems overly thick, add a little more water. Add all other ingredients except kidney beans, lower heat, and cook for 15 minutes.

Add kidney beans and cook for 15 minutes longer. Taste to correct seasonings—the taste for chili powder and cumin is a very individual matter. Remove from heat, cover, and refrigerate.

Before Serving

Cooking Time: 15 min.

Uncover pot and cook on top of stove until heated through, stirring occasionally. It may also be reheated, covered, in a 350° oven for 20 minutes.

Serves 4 or 5

Pot Luck Roast

The glory of this pot roast is in the gravy. And the glory of the gravy is that at some point you're going to run it through your blender so that you can add to it whatever spare vegetables you're hoarding in little dishes in your refrigerator. The few spoonfuls of leftover string beans, the one stalk of celery, and/or the half tomato which you toss in do wondrous things for the flavor of the gravy. For your liquid, use water, bouillon or, preferably, any liquid you have saved from canned vegetables. At least ¼ cup of the liquid, however, should be tomato juice, leftover tomato paste, purée, sauce, or what-have-you with a tomato flavor.

If you're short on available preparation time, you can use small canned potatoes and canned whole carrots. If you do, add them when you warm the pot roast before serving.

1 pot roast, about 3 lbs.	1 cup leftover vegetables (see note above)
3 tablespoons salad oil	
1 medium onion, sliced	2 teaspoons flour
2 cups liquid (see note above)	4 potatoes
1 tablespoon salt	1 bunch carrots

The Night Before

Preparation Time: 30 min.   *Cooking Time:* 2½ hrs.

Heat oil in a large pot or Dutch oven. Add onions and cook slowly until golden but not crisp. Add the pot roast and brown it on all sides. Add the liquid, the salt, and the leftover vegetables. Cover and simmer over low flame for 2½ hrs.

While the onions and meat are browning, peel the carrots and potatoes. Cut the potatoes in half and the carrots in thirds. Cook the two vegetables together in boiling water for 20 min. Drain, cool, and refrigerate.

When the meat has simmered the required time, remove it to a plate. Run all the gravy through the blender, adding the flour. (Be careful not to put more gravy into the blender than it can handle at one time. This gravy is too good to waste in spattering or overflow.) You can add a little Kitchen Bouquet or soy sauce for a deeper color if you're so inclined.

Return the gravy and the meat to the pot. Cover and refrigerate.

Before Serving

Preparation Time: 2 min.   *Cooking Time:* 20 min.

Skim fat from gravy. Add carrots and potatoes. Cover and heat over a low flame for 20 min.   *Serves 5 to 6*

Can be frozen before adding potatoes

Quick Meat Balls in Gravy

This recipe may be a far cry from haute cuisine, but it's pretty good and it can be a lifesaver when you're really rushed and haven't planned ahead. While it is possible to prepare this dish the night before and reheat it before serving, it's so fast and simple that we generally save it for tight spots—those times when you have half an hour to come up with a hot, attractive meal and have had no time to think about it.

1 package instant onion gravy   1½ lbs. ground chuck
    mix   ¼ cup milk
¾ cup water

Preparation Time: 7 min.   *Cooking Time:* 20 min.

Prepare gravy according to package directions, using ¼ cup less water than called for.

While gravy is cooking, form meat into balls. When the gravy has thickened, turn the heat down so that it simmers and gently drop meat balls into gravy. Partially cover pan and cook for 20 minutes, stirring occasionally.

After 20 minutes, stir in ¼ cup milk or more if necessary to give the gravy a pleasing color and consistency. Cook for a minute or two longer to heat through. May be served immediately or refrigerated and reheated.   *Serves 4*

Stuffed Peppers

Most stuffed pepper recipes involve baking the peppers. Any of these can be adapted to night-before preparation by preparing and stuffing the peppers and refrigerating them at the point where your recipe calls for putting them in the oven. This particular recipe (which we would guess is Hungarian in origin) calls for top-of-the-stove cooking, and we like it best of all.

4 large, firm green peppers	2 teaspoons salt
1 lb. chopped chuck	¼ teaspoon Tabasco
¼ cup uncooked rice	3 tablespoons cold water
3 onions, 1 grated and 2 sliced	3 tablespoons salad oil
1 egg, slightly beaten	1 can (1 lb.) stewed tomatoes

. . . .

¼ cup honey	¼ cup lemon juice

The Night Before

Preparation Time: 15 min.   *Cooking Time:* 1 hr., 15 min.

Put the peppers in a large pot, cover with water and bring to a boil. When water reaches the boiling point, turn off the flame and let the peppers stay in the water for 5 min. Drain and cool. Cut the top inch off, saving the tops. Remove the seeds and membranes and rinse the peppers.

While the peppers are being prepared, grate one onion. Mix together the beef, rice, grated onion, beaten egg, salt, Tabasco, and the 3 tablespoons cold water. Stuff the peppers with the mixture and put them aside.

Heat the salad oil in the pot in which the peppers were scalded. Sauté the 2 sliced onions in the oil until golden, but not crisp. Add the stewed tomatoes and then place the peppers (with their tops put back on) over the sauce. Spoon some of the sauce over the peppers. Cover the pot and simmer over a low flame for 1 hr. Cool and refrigerate.

Before Serving

Preparation Time: 2 min.   *Cooking Time:* 30 min.

Add honey and lemon juice to the sauce and stir well. (You can add a little more salt and some pepper to the sauce at this time if you want to.) Simmer over low flame for 30 min.

Serves 4

Chuck Steak Special

This is an ingenious way to make an inexpensive chuck steak taste like something special. Buy enough chuck to feed the number of people you will be serving but use the amounts indicated for the marinade, regardless of the size of the steak. You can, after using it, strain the marinade to remove any meat particles and then refrigerate it for use over and over again.

Chuck steak, cut 2 inches thick, well trimmed
Unsalted meat tenderizer

1 cup dry white vermouth
½ cup soy sauce

The Night Before

Preparation Time: 5 min.

Use meat tenderizer on both sides of steak in accordance with directions on the tenderizer bottle. Mix vermouth and soy sauce and marinate the steak in the mixture, turning once or twice. Cover with aluminum foil and refrigerate. Turn the steak once again before you go to bed and again in the morning.

Before Serving

Preparation Time: 2 min.   *Cooking Time:* 30 min.

Pour off the marinade. Broil the steak, not too close to the flame, for 15 min. on each side. This will give you medium rare meat. Shorten or lengthen the cooking time if you like your meat either very rare or well done.

Hungarian Goulash

3½ cups chopped onions
2 cloves garlic, minced
3 lbs. lean chuck, cut in 2-inch cubes
4 tablespoons bacon fat (or butter)

2 green peppers, coarsely chopped
2½ tablespoons Hungarian paprika
1 tablespoon salt
½ teaspoon pepper
1 8-oz. can tomato sauce

. . . .

1 cup sour cream

The Night Before

Preparation Time: 45 min.   *Cooking Time:* 2 hrs., 15 min.

Chop the onions and garlic. Put 2 tablespoons of the fat in a Dutch oven and sauté the garlic and onions in the fat for 10 minutes, stirring frequently.

Wash, seed, and chop the peppers while the onions are cooking.

Remove the onions from the pot, heat the remaining 2 tablespoons of fat, and brown the meat cubes on all sides. When they are browned, sprinkle the paprika, salt, and pepper over the meat and mix. Return the onions and garlic to the pot and add the chopped green pepper and tomato sauce.

Mix well, cover, and cook over a low flame for 2 hours, 15 minutes. Allow to cool slightly and refrigerate.

Before Serving

Preparation Time: 4 min.   *Cooking Time:* 18 min.

Place pot on a low flame and cook for 15 minutes, stirring occasionally.

Add sour cream and cook, stirring, until the sauce is hot but not boiling.   *Serves 6*

Beef Shishkebab

2 lbs. sirloin, cut in cubes
1 large onion, sliced

1 bay leaf
Enough sherry or burgundy to cover

(Use only two of the following. If you plan to use more, you will need 5 skewers for 4 servings.)

½ lb. fresh mushrooms
1 can boiled onions or 2 medium raw onions

3 large tomatoes or 16 cherry tomatoes
2 green peppers

• • • • • • • • • • •

4 tablespoons melted butter

The Night Before

Preparation Time: 10 min.

Cover the sirloin cubes with the sliced onion, bay leaf, and wine. Cover the dish and refrigerate.

If you are using mushrooms, wash and stem them. If you are using raw onions, peel them and cut in wedges. Peppers should be washed and cut in 2-inch cubes. Refrigerate the vegetables in a plastic bag.

Before Serving

Preparation Time: 12 min.   *Cooking Time:* 17 to 24 min.

Heat broiler. Melt butter in a saucepan. If you are using fresh tomatoes, cut them in wedges. (Cherry tomatoes, of course, remain whole.) Canned onions should be drained.

Place meat and vegetables on 4 large skewers, alternating pieces. Brush with melted butter. Broil 17 min. if you like your meat fairly rare or up to 24 min. if you like it well done. Turn once halfway through broiling and brush with whatever remaining butter you may have.   *Serves 4*

Tacos

People who return to California or Texas after a long absence have been known to go right from the airport to the nearest taco stand—so great is their hunger for what can best be described as a Mexican Big Mac (Big Mex?). The preparation of tacos at home is easiest and most fun if it is turned into a participatory event; the cook sits at the table and has at hand a stack of tortillas, an electric frying pan, and plenty of paper towels; she quickly fries the tortillas and passes them around so people can fill their own with the ingredients arranged on the table. Tacos are great fun for an informal dinner party. And, wonder of wonders, almost all kids love them.

1 package (12) frozen tortillas (not boxed taco shells)
1¼ lb. ground beef
1 clove minced garlic
1 tablespoon (or more) chili powder
2 tablespoons tomato paste
1 teaspoon (or more) salt
1 cup (approximately ½ can) pink beans (*habichuelas rosadas*). If unavailable, use red kidney beans, but the taste isn't quite the same.

½ head lettuce
2 medium-large onions
3 tomatoes
8 ounces Monterey Jack cheese (mild cheddar may be substituted)
1 small can (4 oz.) green chilies (optional)

. . . .

½ to ¾ cup salad oil

The Night Before
Preparation and Cooking Time: 30 min.

Remove tortillas from freezer and place unopened package in refrigerator to thaw overnight.

Brown ground beef and minced garlic in saucepan until the meat is no longer red. Pour off fat.

Add chili powder, tomato paste, and salt; cook together for 5 minutes over low heat.

Purée beans in blender (or mash with a fork if you do not have a blender) and add to meat mixture. Cook for 10 minutes over low to medium heat.

Taste to correct seasonings. Mexican food fans will want *much* more chili powder and perhaps some more pureed beans. If the mixture is not very thick, add a little more tomato paste. Remove from heat, cover, and refrigerate.

While the meat is cooking, you can prepare the garnishes. Cut the lettuce into thin shreds (like cole slaw), chop the onions, dice the tomatoes, chop the green chilies, and grate the cheese, using a grater that will result in very finely grated cheese. Place each garnish into a separate plastic bag or covered dish and refrigerate.

Before Serving

Preparation Time: 5 min.   *Cooking Time:* 15 min.

Heat beef mixture on top of stove until very hot.

Arrange lettuce, tomatoes, cheese, onions, and chilies on a serving dish and place on table.

At table, pour salad oil into electric frying pan to a depth of ¼ inch. Place tortillas and paper towels nearby.

When ready to serve, turn control on electric frying pan to the highest setting. After everyone is seated, place the hot meat mixture on the table and proceed as follows:

Using tongs, place two or three tortillas into the hot oil. Fry for just a few seconds, turn and fry a few seconds more, and remove. The tortillas should be crisp at the edges but still pliable so they can be folded in half. Pat dry on paper towels, fold in half, and pass to the diners.

Each person concocts his own taco, using the ingredients on the table, in this order:

meat mixture
grated cheese
onions
tomatoes
lettuce
green chilies

Serves 4 to 6
Meat mixture can be frozen

Beef with Oyster Sauce

The only slightly unusual ingredient in this fast, delicious dish is the oyster sauce, which can be bought in a bottle at many gourmet food stores, at Japanese and Chinese food stores, or by mail from one of the sources on page 12. The unused portion can be kept refrigerated for months.

The recipe also calls for fresh ginger; no substitution of powdered ginger will quite do the trick. This can be bought not only from the sources indicated for the oyster sauce, but usually also in Mexican and Latin American food stores as well. It, too, can be kept for months: peel the ginger, put the chunks into a small jar, cover with sherry, and refrigerate.

If your friendly butcher will cut the steak stroganoff style for you, you can start out with strips of meat the proper size. Otherwise, buy a piece of boneless sirloin, put it in the freezer briefly to chill, and slice it in ¼-inch strips.

We recommend that you serve this with rice, vermicelli, or perhaps with the nice fast-cooking dried shrimp noodles that you'll find in oriental food stores.

If you haven't been discouraged by the length of all these introductory hints, take cheer—it will take you less time to cook the meal than it took to read all this!

3 scallions, diced	¼ teaspoon pepper
1½ lbs. sirloin, cut in ¼-inch strips	¼ cup oyster sauce
	½ cup chicken broth
2 tablespoons soy sauce	⅛ teaspoon salt
2 tablespoons sherry	1 tablespoon cornstarch
1 tablespoon oil	1 clove garlic, minced
1 teaspoon sugar	2 slices ginger, crushed
1 teaspoon MSG	

. . . .

2 tablespoons peanut oil

The Night Before

Preparation Time: 10 min.

Wash and dice scallions and refrigerate in a small plastic bag.

Mix the soy sauce, sherry, oil, sugar, MSG, and pepper and pour the mixture over the steak, turning the meat to coat well. Refrigerate, covered.

Mix the oyster sauce, chicken broth, salt, and cornstarch and refrigerate in a small jar or covered cup.

Mince the garlic and flatten the ginger slices with the back of a cleaver or heavy knife. Refrigerate in a plastic bag.

Before Serving

Preparation and Cooking Time: 8 min.

Heat a regular or electric wok or a skillet (375° if you're using an electric appliance).

Pour the oil into the heated pan. When it is hot, add the garlic and ginger and stir-fry briefly until the garlic turns golden. Add the steak and cook, turning frequently, until all the meat is browned.

Remove the meat from the pan, discard the ginger, and add the scallions to the pan. Cook for about ½ minute, stirring.

Thoroughly stir the soy sauce-sherry mixture. Add this to the pan and cook, stirring until the sauce is thickened.

Replace beef in the pan and stir-fry just until beef is reheated and well coated with sauce. *Serves 4*

Beef and Snow Peas

This fast, delicious Chinese dish can be made in a wok or an electric frying pan or any large skillet. It will take just a bit longer if you're not using a wok since the curved sides of the wok provide a larger cooking surface. Whichever utensil you use, the dish won't take you more than 10 minutes to prepare.

If you can't buy (or grow) fresh snow peas, you can use the easily available frozen ones provided you thaw and dry them thoroughly. The fresh ones are crisper and well worth a little effort to get.

½ lb. fresh or 1 package frozen snow peas
1 clove garlic, minced
2 slices fresh ginger, crushed (see note on page 11)
2 tablespoons soy sauce
3 tablespoons cold water

1 teaspoon sugar
1 teaspoon MSG (monosodium glutamate)
1 tablespoon cornstarch
¼ teaspoon salt
2 tablespoons sherry
½ cup chicken broth

. . . .

1 lb. sirloin, sliced stroganoff style (see note on page 36)

3 tablespoons peanut oil

The Night Before

Preparation Time: 10 min.

If you're using fresh snow peas, pull off the stem end of each pea and the side string that usually comes off with it. Rinse and drain thoroughly between layers of paper towel. If you're using frozen ones, thaw and dry them in paper towels. Put dry snow peas in a plastic bag and refrigerate.

Mince garlic. Crush the 2 slices of ginger by pounding with the back of a cleaver or large knife. Put the garlic and ginger in plastic wrap and refrigerate.

Mix the soy cause, water, sugar, MSG, and cornstarch in a small cup or jar. Cover and refrigerate.

Mix the chicken broth, sherry, and salt in another cup or jar. Cover and refrigerate.

Before Serving

Preparation and Cooking Time: 10 min.

Take the sliced steak, the two jars, the snow peas, and the garlic-ginger package out of the refrigerator and put them close by your wok or skillet.

Heat wok or skillet. Add 1 tablespoon oil. As soon as it is hot, add the garlic and ginger and stir briefly until the garlic is golden but not burned.

Add the beef, stirring with two large spoons or spatulas until it is browned. Transfer the contents of the pan to a bowl.

Put the remaining 2 tablespoons of oil in the pan. When hot, add the snow peas and cook, stirring, until they have turned a darker green. (They should still be firm, not soft; this will take 1 to 2 minutes.)

Replace the beef in the pan and add the contents of the jar that holds the sherry-broth combination. Stir well.

Mix the contents of the other jar with a spoon to be sure the cornstarch isn't sticking to the bottom of the jar. Add this mixture to the pan and stir until the gravy is thickened.

Remove the ginger slices. Serve the beef with rice or noodles.

Serves 4

Glazed Corned Beef

3 lbs. corned beef brisket
1 peeled carrot
1 onion, quartered

1 teaspoon salt
Dash of pepper

. . . .

2 tablespoons prepared mustard
¼ cup maple syrup

2 tablespoons dark brown sugar

The Night Before

Preparation Time: 10 min.   *Cooking Time:* 3 hrs.

Place corned beef, carrot, onion, salt, and pepper in large saucepan with enough water to cover. Bring to boil and then simmer over a medium flame for 3 hrs. or until beef seems tender. Remove beef from water and let cool. Wrap in foil and refrigerate.

Before Serving

Preparation Time: 10 min.   *Cooking Time:* 18 min.

While broiler is heating, combine mustard, syrup, and brown sugar in a small saucepan. Bring to the boiling point, then reduce heat and simmer for 5 min., stirring frequently. Brush the glazing sauce over the corned beef and put beef in broiler, 5 or 6 inches from heat. Broil for 10 min., brushing two or three times with the remaining glaze. Slice and serve.

Serves 4

Italian Pot Roast

4 lbs. pot roast
½ teaspoon salt
½ teaspoon pepper
2 cloves garlic, cut into slivers
½ cup flour
¼ cup olive oil

1 cup tomato juice
1 large carrot, sliced
2 onions, chopped
2 teaspoons oregano
½ teaspoon basil
1 cup tomato purée

. . . .

3 tablespoons chopped parsley

The Night Before

Preparation Time: 20 min.   *Cooking Time:* 2 hrs.

Rub meat with salt and pepper. Make tiny, deep incisions on all sides of the meat with the point of a knife and push a sliver of garlic into each cut. Roll meat in flour. Heat olive oil in deep, heavy pot and, over high heat, brown meat on all sides. While meat is browning, peel and chop onion, scrape and slice carrot, and measure out other ingredients. When meat is brown, lower heat and add tomato juice, carrot, onion, basil, and oregano. Cover and simmer gently for 1¼ hrs.

After 1¼ hrs., add tomato purée and stir through. Simmer for 45 min. longer. Remove from heat, let stand for 15 min., then refrigerate, covered.

Before Serving

Preparation Time: 3 min.   *Cooking Time:* 20 min.

Discard fat that has congealed on surface of sauce. Place covered pot on top of stove and simmer until meat is hot—about 20 min. Just before serving, chop parsley (if you haven't already done so) and stir into sauce.   *Serves 6 to 8*
Can be frozen after slicing

Boeuf Bourguignon

3 tablespoons salad oil
2 lbs. lean beef chuck, cut in cubes
2 tablespoons flour
1 teaspoon salt

¼ teaspoon pepper
¼ teaspoon thyme
1 cup undiluted beef broth
1 cup Burgundy

. . . .

1 (3 oz.) can mushrooms   1 small can white onions

The Night Before

Preparation Time: 20 to 25 min.   *Cooking Time:* 2½ hrs.

Heat salad oil in skillet or electric frying pan. Brown meat on all sides. While meat is browning, heat oven to 325°. When meat is browned, stir in flour, salt, pepper, and thyme. Mix well with meat, scraping bottom of pan. Put everything in a 3-quart casserole.

Mix beef broth and wine and pour over meat. Place covered casserole in oven and bake for 2½ hrs. Cool slightly and refrigerate.

Before Serving

Preparation Time: 5 min.   *Cooking Time:* 35 min.

Heat oven to 325°. If the liquid has evaporated, broth and wine may be added in equal parts. (This shouldn't be necessary if your oven keeps a proper temperature.) Add drained mushrooms and onions. Stir, cover, and bake for 35 min.

Serves 4

Can be frozen

Corned Beef or Roast Beef Hash

Hash is simple, hearty, satisfying, and so old-fashioned that many cooks seem to have forgotten all about it in the constant search for something new and different. Next time you have a roast-beef-and-potatoes dinner or prepare corned beef with cabbage and boiled potatoes, plan to serve hash later in the week—if yours is like most families, your kids have never tasted it and your husband has not eaten it in years. They'll probably love it.

2 to 3 cups cooked roast beef or corned beef
4 boiled or baked potatoes
1 onion

. . . .

3 tablespoons bacon fat or cooking oil
salt and pepper

The Night Before

Preparation Time: 12 min.

Dice meat and potatoes (left over from another meal) and refrigerate in a plastic bag.

Chop onion and refrigerate in a separate plastic bag.

Before Serving

Preparation Time: 5 min.   *Cooking Time:* 30 min.

Melt bacon fat or heat oil in large frying pan. Add chopped onions and cook over medium high heat just until onions soften —about 2 or 3 minutes.

Add meat and potatoes and stir. Lower heat and cook for 30 minutes; turn mixture with a spatula several times as it cooks. Season to taste with salt and pepper.   *Serves 4*

Swedish Meat Balls and Gravy

MEAT BALLS

1 lb. finely ground chuck
2 slices white bread
¼ cup milk
1 small onion, grated
1 egg

1 tablespoon parsley, finely
    chopped
¼ teaspoon ground cloves
¼ teaspoon ground allspice
4 tablespoons (half stick) butter

GRAVY

2 tablespoons flour
1½ cups canned beef broth
¼ to ½ teaspoon soy sauce

1 teaspoon Worcestershire
    sauce
Salt and pepper

The Night Before
Preparation and Cooking Time: 18 min.

Soak bread in milk, then use your hands to mix the two together until the mixture has the consistency of a thick batter. Add meat, onion, egg, parsley, cloves, and allspice, and mix thoroughly. Shape into tiny balls. Melt butter in a large skillet and brown meat balls on all sides. Remove meat balls from skillet with slotted spoon.

Thicken butter remaining in skillet with flour. Slowly add beef broth, Worcestershire sauce, and ¼ teaspoon soy sauce. Cook over low heat, stirring until thickened and smooth. Taste to see if you want to add another ¼ teaspoon soy sauce and/or salt and pepper.

Place meat balls in gravy, cover, and refrigerate.

Before Serving
Cooking Time: 10 min.

Cook, covered, over medium-low heat for 10 min., or until heated through.   *Serves 4*

□ LAMB □

Teriyaki Lamb Chops

6 to 8 shoulder lamb chops
3 cloves garlic
1 teaspoon powdered ginger or
    1 tablespoon minced fresh
    ginger

⅓ cup soy sauce
2 tablespoons molasses
1 teaspoon dry mustard
½ cup orange marmalade
½ cup white vinegar

. . . .

2 tablespoons cornstarch

¼ cup cold water

The Night Before
Preparation and Cooking Time: 12 min.

Brown the chops lightly on both sides in a large skillet (350° if electric).

While the chops are browning, mince the garlic (and the ginger if you're using fresh ginger) and mix these with all remaining ingredients above the dotted line.

If your skillet can be put in the refrigerator, pour the sauce over the chops and cover and refrigerate. Otherwise, remove the chops to another dish and refrigerate the chops and the sauce separately.

Before Serving
Preparation Time: 3 min.   *Cooking Time:* 25 min.

Put the chops back in the skillet if you removed them and pour the sauce over them.

Cook, covered, for 25 minutes (at 300° if using electric skillet), turning once and spooning sauce over chops.

Mix the cornstarch and cold water. When the chops are done, remove them to a platter and add the cornstarch mixture to the sauce in the pan. Cook, stirring, for a minute or so until the sauce is thickened.

Spoon sauce over chops and serve.   *Serves 4*

Curried Meatballs

MEATBALLS

1½ lbs. ground lamb—some su-
    permarkets sell this as
    "lamb patties"
2 cloves garlic, minced
1 egg

½ cup pignoli (pine nuts)
⅓ cup finely chopped parsley
¾ teaspoon salt
4 tablespoons olive oil

CURRY SAUCE

6 tablespoons butter or
    margarine
2 stalks celery, diced
1 large apple, cored and diced
    (unpeeled)

1 large onion, diced
2 to 3 teaspoons curry powder
2 cups tomato juice
¼ cup tomato paste

. . . .

scant tablespoonful chutney

The Night Before

Preparation and Cooking Time: 25 min.

Heat oven to 350°.

Combine lamb, garlic, egg, nuts, parsley, and salt and mix thoroughly. Then add olive oil and mix again. Form into 1-inch balls and place in shallow pan.

Bake meatballs for 15 minutes—they should be well browned on the outside but medium rare in the center.

While meatballs are baking, prepare curry sauce. Melt the butter in a 2-quart pot—one that also can be used as a serving dish. Add the diced celery, apple, and onion. Cook over low heat until celery softens and onion becomes translucent. Stir in curry powder, starting with 2 teaspoons and increasing according to taste; cook very gently for 5 minutes longer. Add tomato juice and cook over medium heat for 5 minutes. Stir in tomato paste to thicken sauce.

Add meatballs to sauce, cover, and refrigerate.

Before Serving

Preparation Time: 1 min.   *Cooking Time:* 15 min.

Cook, covered, on top of stove over medium-low heat until heated through—about 15 minutes.

Remove from heat and stir in chutney. Serve over boiled white rice.

Serves 4

Lamb Marengo

3 lbs. lamb necks for stewing	1 clove garlic, crushed or finely
½ cup salad oil	chopped
2 tablespoons butter	1 bay leaf
2 onions, chopped	1 tablespoon salt
1 teaspoon flour	4 tablespoons sherry
2 (6 oz.) cans tomato paste	1 cup water

· · · · · · · · · · · ·

1 lb. small fresh mushrooms, or
1 (6 oz.) can mushrooms

The Night Before

Preparation Time: 20 min.   *Cooking Time:* 1½ hrs.

Heat oil and butter in large skillet. Fry meat briskly until well browned on all sides. Add onions and cook until transparent. Add flour, stirring it in as evenly as possible. Add all other ingredients, *except mushrooms,* and blend well.

Reduce heat, cover, and cook gently for 1½ hours. Remove from heat, allow to cool, and refrigerate, covered.

Before Serving

Preparation Time: 5 min.   *Cooking Time:* 30 min.

Wipe mushrooms with damp cloth, or rinse in cold water. If canned mushrooms are used, drain them and set aside.

Over low heat, cook the meat and sauce for 15 min., stirring occasionally. Add mushrooms and cook for 15 min. longer.

Serves 4

Devonshire Pie

3 tablespoons butter
¼ cup celery, finely minced
1 tablespoon flour
1½ cups hot water
1½ teaspoons beef bouillon
    powder
1¼ lbs. lean boned lamb, cut in
    1″ cubes

3 apples
2 medium onions
1 tablespoon brown sugar
1 tablespoon cinnamon
salt and pepper

. . . .

1 frozen pie shell

The Night Before

Preparation Time: 35 min.　　　　　　*Cooking Time:* 35 min.

Mince the celery. Melt 1 tablespoon of the butter in a small saucepan and sauté the celery for about 2 minutes over a medium flame. Add the flour and mix, stirring constantly until flour browns. Add water and bouillon powder and cook over a low flame for 15 minutes, stirring occasionally. Set sauce aside.

Brown the lamb in the remaining 2 tablespoons of butter.

Peel, core, and slice the apples and cut the onions in thin slices.

In a 2-quart casserole, place half the lamb in a single layer. Top this with a layer of apples and sprinkle half the sugar and cinnamon over the apples. Top with a layer of onions, then the rest of the meat, another layer of onions, and a top layer of apples sprinkled with the remaining sugar and cinnamon.

Pour the sauce mixture into the casserole. Cover and bake at 350° for 35 minutes. Refrigerate, covered.

Before Serving

Preparation Time: 5 min.　　　　　　*Cooking Time:* 35 to 40 min.

Heat oven to 425°. Take the pie shell out of the freezer and let it stand at room temperature for 10 minutes.

Remove the cover from the lamb casserole and replace it

with the pie crust topping. With a small knife, make 3 or 4 slits in the top of the crust to let steam escape.

Bake 35 to 40 minutes, until top is well browned.   *Serves 4*

Rancho Riblets

3 lbs. lamb riblets, cut in individual ribs
1 onion
2 cloves garlic
½ cup ketchup
½ cup water
¼ cup cider vinegar
1 tablespoon Worcestershire
sauce
⅛ teaspoon Tabasco
2 teaspoons salt
1 teaspoon chili powder

The Night Before

Preparation Time: 20 min.   *Cooking Time:* 1 hr.

In a large skillet or heavy pot, brown the riblets. As they brown, remove them to a casserole that can go both on top of the stove and in the oven. Discard the fat in the browning pan.

While the riblets are browning, slice the onion and mince the garlic. Mix all remaining ingredients together with the onion and garlic.

Pour the sauce over the riblets, cover the casserole, and simmer over a moderate flame for 1 hour.

With tongs, remove the riblets from the sauce and refrigerate them, covered. Re-cover the sauce and refrigerate it separately. (This will make it easier to remove the fat from the sauce before serving.)

Before Serving

Preparation Time: 3 min.   *Cooking Time:* 30 min.

Heat oven to 350°.

With a large spoon, skim the fat off the top of the sauce. Replace the riblets in the skimmed sauce.

Bake, uncovered, for ½ hour.   *Serves 4*
Can be frozen

Shepherd's Pie

We've never been able to figure out where people get all those leftovers that appear to create a frantic need for recipes on the subject. On the rare occasions when we have leftovers, they seem to take care of themselves with the aid of midnight refrigerator raiders and certain members of our somewhat eccentric families who consider last night's leftovers infinitely more interesting than bacon and eggs for breakfast.

As a result, we find that we almost have to create our leftovers intentionally. If you cook a little more lamb or pot roast or such than you'll need for the meal you're planning and squirrel a bit of it away in the freezer where it isn't subject to impulse snacking, you'll have your base for Shepherd's Pie.

One word about the meat stock: you can use 1½ cups of hot water into which you stir a heaping teaspoon of Bovril or some similar beef base. If you have leftover gravy, by all means use it, but if you do, cut down on the amount of flour specified by this recipe if your gravy is already thick.

You can cut the preparation time by substituting instant mashed potatoes. If you do, don't add them the night before. Prepare them according to package directions while your oven is heating the night you're serving the dish.

4 medium potatoes (about 1½ lbs.)
¼ cup chopped onion
¼ cup chopped green pepper
½ cup diced celery
3 tablespoons butter or chicken fat
3 tablespoons flour
1½ cups meat stock (see note above)

1¼–1½ cups diced cooked meat
½ cup cooked carrots, peas, or any other leftover or canned vegetable
⅓ cup milk
2 tablespoons butter or chicken fat
1 teaspoon salt
¼ teaspoon white pepper

. . . .

2 tablespoons butter or chicken fat

The Night Before

Preparation Time: 25 min.   Cooking Time: 20 min.

Boil a pot of water. Peel potatoes, cut them in quarters, and cook in boiling salted water for 20 minutes.

Dice onion, pepper, and celery and sauté them in the 3 tablespoons of fat until tender. Add the flour and stir. Add the meat stock, meat, and carrots or other vegetable and allow the mixture to cook slowly for 5 minutes until the gravy has thickened. (You can add a bit of Kitchen Bouquet at this point for color if you like.) Remove the mixture to a greased 1-quart casserole.

Put the cooked potatoes in the bowl of your electric mixer or mash them thoroughly by hand, adding the milk, 2 tablespoons of butter or chicken fat, and the salt and pepper.

Top the meat casserole with a layer of the mashed potatoes. Cover and refrigerate.

Before Serving

Preparation Time: 2 min.   Cooking Time: 35 min.

Heat the oven to 400°. While it is heating, melt the 2 tablespoons of butter or chicken fat and brush the melted fat over the top of the potato topping.

Bake, uncovered, for 35 minutes or until top is nicely browned.   *Serves 4*

Versatile Lamb Stew

We call this stew versatile because it can be made with either uncooked or leftover cooked lamb. In fact, it can consist of a combination of leftover meats that you have accumulated in the freezer. We try to save a large chunk of Sunday's leg of lamb to use for this recipe a few days later—no one has ever even whispered the word "leftover."

2 onions
2 cloves garlic
2 tablespoons butter or margarine
3 tablespoons vegetable oil
2½ lbs. lamb shoulder, cut in 1½-inch cubes, or 4 cups cooked leftover lamb, cut in 1½-inch cubes

3 tablespoons flour
1½ cups dry red wine
1½ cups beef bouillon
3 tablespoons tomato paste
1 teaspoon salt
¼ teaspoon pepper
½ teaspoon rosemary
½ lb. mushrooms

. . . .

2 tablespoons butter

The Night Before
Preparation Time: 17 min.   *Cooking Time:* 1 hr.

Slice onion into rings, mince garlic. Heat butter or margarine in frying pan and sauté onion and garlic until golden.

In large casserole, heat oil until very hot. Toss meat in oil until lightly browned. Add flour and cook, stirring briskly, just until flour begins to brown. Lower heat and add all other ingredients except mushrooms. The liquid should just about cover the meat; if it does not, add a little more beef bouillon. Cover and simmer for 1 hour, stirring occasionally. Refrigerate.

Slice mushrooms and refrigerate in plastic bag.

Before Serving
Preparation Time: 7 min.   *Cooking Time:* 15 min.

Place covered casserole on stove and cook for about 15 minutes, or until heated through.

Meanwhile, heat butter in frying pan and sauté mushrooms

in butter for about 5 minutes. Just before serving stew, stir in mushrooms.

Serves 6

Irish Stew

The really nice thing about the traditional Irish stew is that everything goes into one pot at one time—no need to flour or pre-brown the meat.

3 lbs. potatoes	salt
4 onions	pepper
4 carrots	2½ cups beef broth
2 lbs. cubed lamb shoulder	1 bay leaf

The Night Before

Preparation Time: 10 min.   *Cooking Time:* 2 hrs., 15 min.

Pare potatoes and slice them into rounds. Peel onions and slice into circles. Scrape and slice carrots.

Layer meat, onions, carrots, and potatoes in a deep, heavy pot that can be used on top of the stove and in the oven. Sprinkle each layer with a little salt and pepper. End with a layer of potatoes.

Pour the beef broth into the pot—it should just cover the top layer of potatoes; adjust amount accordingly. Add the bay leaf.

Cook over fairly high heat until broth boils. Then turn heat very low and cook covered, for 2 hours and 15 minutes. Remove bay leaf, cover, and refrigerate.

Before Serving

Preparation Time: 1 min.   *Cooking Time:* 20 min.

Heat oven to 350°.

Bake, covered, for about 20 minutes or until heated through.

Serves 6
Can be frozen

California Lamb Shanks

If you don't happen to have any port on hand, you can marinate the fruit in Cherry Heering or a fruit liqueur or red wine—or even apple juice if you feel so inclined. We like the port best.

1 box mixed dried fruit
½ cup port (see note above)
4 lamb shanks
garlic salt
pepper

2 tablespoons flour
2 tablespoons butter
¼ cup sugar
1 teaspoon cinnamon

The Night Before

Preparation Time: 12 min.   *Cooking Time:* 1 hr., 45 min.

Early in the evening (or in the morning if you prefer) put the fruit in a 3- or 4-quart casserole and pour the port over it. It should marinate for about 2 hours but it won't hurt a bit if you let it stand all day.

Heat oven to 350°.

Sprinkle the lamb shanks generously with garlic salt and pepper and then with the flour.

Melt the butter in a skillet or pot large enough to hold all the shanks. Brown them in the butter.

Add the sugar, cinnamon, and 3 cups of water to the marinated fruit. Mix and then add the lamb shanks, placing some of the fruit and sauce over each piece of meat.

Cover the casserole and bake for 1½ hours. Refrigerate.

Before Serving

Preparation Time: 1 min.   *Cooking Time:* 30 min.

Heat oven to 350°. Spoon sauce and fruit over meat and re-cover casserole.

Bake for 30 minutes.

Serves 4
Can be frozen

Tropical Fruit Lamb

3 tablespoons olive oil
2 lbs. lean lamb, cut in 1-inch pieces
½ cup orange juice
¼ cup lime juice
4 teaspoons cornstarch

¾ cup dry white wine
2 teaspoons salt
½ teaspoon white pepper
2 cloves garlic, minced
¼ cup golden raisins
1 large orange

The Night Before

Preparation Time: 30 min.   *Cooking Time:* 1 hr., 10 min.

Heat the olive oil and brown the lamb bits, turning frequently.

While the lamb is browning, mix the orange juice, lime juice, and cornstarch together. Peel the orange, discarding the white inside of the peel. Grate the peel in an electric blender.

When the lamb is browned, remove it to a small casserole. Discard the fat from the pan in which the lamb was browned and add the wine, stirring at the bottom of the pan to get any browned bits of meat. Add the orange and lime juice mixture, salt and pepper, and cook, stirring, until the sauce is thickened.

Remove the sauce from the heat, add the garlic and raisins, and pour the sauce over the lamb. Mix well, cover, and bake at 350° for 1 hour. Allow to cool slightly, cover and refrigerate.

Cut the peeled orange in thin slices, wrap in plastic wrap and refrigerate.

Before Serving

Preparation Time: 5 min.   *Cooking Time:* 40 min.

Heat oven to 350°.

Remove any fat from the top of the dish. Mix with a large spoon. Place the reserved slices of orange on top and cover the casserole.

Bake, covered, for 40 minutes.

Serves 4
Can be frozen

Kafta

1½ lbs. ground lamb
1 medium onion, chopped fine
2 cups parsley, chopped fine
2 tablespoons butter

3 heaping tablespoons pignolia
  (pine nuts)
1¼ teaspoons salt
⅛ teaspoon pepper

· · · · · · · · · · · · ·

1 can (1 lb.) stewed tomatoes

The Night Before

Preparation Time: 15 min.   *Cooking Time:* 12 min.

Mix the lamb, onion, parsley, pignolia, salt, and pepper lightly but thoroughly. Your hands will do this job better than any utensil. Divide the meat into 8 cakes, no more than ¾ inch thick. Sauté in butter over a low flame (300° in an electric skillet) for 10 to 12 minutes. Arrange the meat cakes in a shallow oven dish. Cover and refrigerate.

Before Serving

Preparation Time: 2 min.   *Cooking Time:* 30 min.

Pour the stewed tomatoes over the meat cakes. Bake (uncovered) at 325° for 30 min.   *Serves 4*

Barbecued Lamb and Bean Casserole

1¾ lbs. lean boneless lamb
  shoulder, cut in chunks
½ teaspoon ground allspice
1 onion, sliced
1 stalk celery, sliced
2 tablespoons parsley, minced

1 large tomato, diced
1 small green pepper, diced
1 cup bottled barbecue sauce
1 can 1-lb. vegetarian baked
  beans

The Night Before

Preparation Time: 15 min.   *Cooking Time:* 45 min.

Heat oven to 400°. Place meat in a casserole and sprinkle with the allspice. Bake, uncovered, for 45 minutes, turning the meat 2 or 3 times to allow all surfaces to brown.

While the meat is roasting, slice the onion and celery, mince the parsley, and dice the tomato and green pepper. Mix all the ingredients in a bowl.

When the meat is finished, pour the bean mixture into the casserole, mix well, cover, and refrigerate.

Before Serving

Preparation Time: 1 min.   *Cooking Time:* 1 hr.

Heat oven to 350°.

Mix the casserole once more and bake, covered, for 1 hour.

Serves 4

Lamb Shishkebab

2 lbs. boned leg of lamb, cut in cubes	½ cup lemon juice
	½ cup lime juice
1 #2 can boiled onions	½ cup olive oil
1 green pepper, cut in cubes	1½ teaspoons salt

The Night Before

Preparation Time: 12 min.

Thread the lamb cubes, onions, and green pepper alternately on four long skewers. Lay skewers flat in a large roasting pan.

Combine all other ingredients and mix well. Pour over the filled skewers. Cover pan with foil and refrigerate. Turn skewers once, several hours later or the next morning.

Before Serving

Preparation Time: 3 min.   *Cooking Time:* 20 to 30 min.

Broil the filled skewers about 4 in. from heat for 10 to 15 min., depending on how well done you like your meat. Turn and brush with marinade again and broil for another 10 to 15 min.

Serves 4

Kusa Mihshi: Stuffed Squash in the Lebanese Manner

(This same recipe can be used for stuffing eggplant; substitute 2 medium eggplants for the 6 squash.)

6 yellow crookneck squash
½ lb. ground lamb or beef
1 cup raw white rice
½ cup (1 stick) butter, melted
1 teaspoon salt

¼ teaspoon pepper
1 teaspoon cinnamon
1 can (1 lb.) tomatoes or tomato purée, mixed with 1 can water

The Night Before

Preparation Time: 13 min.   *Cooking Time:* 45 min.

Cut off the "necks" of the squash. (Don't discard them—you can cook and serve them as plain old squash.) Scoop the squash and seeds from the rounded parts, leaving as thin a shell as possible—a melon ball cutter does this nicely. (The scooped-out squash may *also* be cooked as plain old squash.)

Combine meat, rice, melted butter, salt, pepper, and cinnamon. Mix thoroughly. Spoon filling lightly—don't pack it down—into squash shells. The shells should be only two thirds full. Place in a deep, heavy pot. Mix tomato purée or tomatoes and water. Pour into and over stuffed squash. Cover and simmer gently for 45 min. Refrigerate.

Before Serving

Preparation Time: 1 min.   *Cooking Time:* 15 min.

Place pot, still covered, on top of stove and simmer gently for 15 min. Baste squash once or twice with sauce in pot.

Serves 3 to 4 as a main course

Parsley Lamb with String Beans

If you like Shepherd's Pie (page 50), this is a good time to make more lamb than you will need for this meal. Cut 1 to 1½ cups of the extra cooked lamb and save 1½ cups of the liquid for refrigeration or freezing as the basis for Shepherd's Pie at some later date.

1½ lbs. boned lamb, cut in 1½-inch cubes	½ teaspoon pepper
	3 lemon slices
1 tablespoon butter	2 cups water
1½ cups chopped parsley	1 lb. fresh string beans
2 teaspoons salt	

The Night Before

Preparation Time: 20 min.   *Cooking Time:* 1 hr., 10 min.

Brown the lamb cubes in the butter. While they are browning, chop the parsley and slice the lemon.

Add all ingredients except the string beans to the browned lamb. Cover and simmer for 1 hour.

Cut the tips off the string beans and cut them in 2 or 3 pieces (depending on how long they are.) Wash and set them aside.

When the lamb has simmered for 1 hour, remove from stove, add string beans, cover and refrigerate.

Before Serving

Preparation Time: 1 min.   *Cooking Time:* 35 min.

Mix contents of pot, bring to a boil, then reduce heat and simmer, covered, for ½ hour.

Serves 4
Can be frozen

Lamb with Baked Brown Rice

½ cup flour
½ teaspoon salt
¼ teaspoon pepper
2 lbs. boneless lamb shoulder,
    cut in ¾″ cubes

¼ cup olive oil
1 onion
1 clove garlic
1 cup beef broth
½ teaspoon oregano

. . . .

3 cups beef broth

1 cup brown rice

The Night Before

Preparation Time: 23 min.   *Cooking Time:* 1 hr.

Place flour, salt, and pepper in a paper bag. Add cubed lamb and shake until all pieces are well coated with flour.

Heat olive oil in a large, heavy skillet. Chop onion coarsely. Split garlic clove. Sauté onion and garlic in olive oil until onion is soft, then remove onion and garlic with slotted spoon. Set aside.

Cook lamb cubes in olive oil until they are well browned. Add 1 cup of beef broth and bring to a boil. Lower heat and add onion, garlic, and oregano. Cover and simmer for 1 hour.

Remove the two pieces of garlic, cover, and refrigerate.

Before Serving

Preparation Time: 10 min.   *Cooking Time:* 1 hr.

Heat oven to 375°.

Heat lamb on top of stove until warm. Add 3 cups of beef broth and bring to the boiling point.

Place raw brown rice in a 4-quart casserole. Add lamb and broth. Cover and bake for 1 hour.   *Serves 4 to 5*

Lamb Stew with Dumplings

2 lbs. lean shoulder of lamb, cut
    in 2-inch cubes
1 large onion, sliced
¼ cup salad oil
1½ teaspoons salt
1 teaspoon paprika

¼ teaspoon basil
1 garlic clove, chopped
6 carrots, cut in 1-inch cubes
1 can (8 oz.) small boiled
    onions

· · · · · · · · · · · · ·

1 can (1 lb.) small white po-
    tatoes
1 can (13½ oz.) beef bouillon

1 cup Bisquick
3 oz. milk
1 teaspoon parsley flakes

The Night Before
Preparation and Cooking Time: 20 min.

Heat the salad oil in a large skillet. Cook the sliced onion until slightly soft. Add the lamb cubes and brown on all sides. With a slotted spoon, remove the onion and the lamb from the skillet and transfer to a large stove-to-table casserole. Add the salt, paprika, basil, garlic, carrots, and boiled onions to the casserole and mix gently. Cover and refrigerate.

Before Serving
Preparation Time: 6 min.   *Cooking Time:* 1 hr.

Add the drained potatoes and the beef bouillon to the casserole. Stir. Cover and simmer over medium flame. Mix Bisquick, milk, and parsley flakes with a fork. When the stew has simmered for 40 min., top the bubbling stew with spoonfuls of the dumpling mixture. Cook, uncovered, for 10 min.; then cover and cook for 10 min. more.   *Serves 4*

Moussaka

You can use 5 cups of the basic meat sauce on page 18 for this dish, in which case you'll save the time indicated below for the preparation of the meat sauce.

MEAT SAUCE

3 tomatoes
2 large onions, minced
1 clove garlic, minced
¼ cup parsley, minced
2 tablespoons butter

2 lbs. lean ground beef or lamb
8 oz. can tomato sauce
½ teaspoon cinnamon
1 tablespoon salt

MOUSSAKA

3 medium eggplants
salt

8 tablespoons butter

. . . .

2 tablespoons butter
¼ cup flour
2 cups milk
1½ teaspoons salt

dash of nutmeg
1 cup ricotta cheese
3 beaten eggs

The Night Before

The Meat Sauce
Preparation Time: 30 min.   *Cooking Time:* 30 min.

Plunge the tomatoes into boiling water for one minute. Rinse with cold water and remove skins. Dice.

Chop onion, garlic, and parsley.

Melt the 2 tablespoons of butter and sauté the onions until wilted but not browned. Add the meat and garlic and cook, stirring, until meat is all browned.

Add the diced tomatoes, tomato sauce, parsley, salt, and cinnamon and cook for ½ hour or until almost all liquid has disappeared.

The Moussaka
Preparation and Cooking Time: 40 min.

Pare eggplants and cut lengthwise in half-inch slices. Sprinkle generously with salt and set aside for 15 minutes. Pour off any liquid that has accumulated and dry the eggplant slices thoroughly on paper towels.

Using about 2 tablespoons of butter for each batch, brown the eggplant slices on both sides over a medium flame (350° if you're using an electric skillet).

If you're using your supply of Basic Meat Sauce, warm it slightly, adding ½ teaspoon cinnamon.

Put a layer of half the eggplant slices in a 13" x 9" x 2" baking dish. Top with half the meat sauce, then with the remaining eggplant and the rest of the meat sauce. Cover and refrigerate.

Before Serving

Preparation Time: 5 min.   *Cooking Time:* 50 min.

Heat oven to 375°.

Melt 2 tablespoons butter in a saucepan. Add flour and cook 1 minute, stirring constantly. Add the milk, salt, and nutmeg. Bring to a boil and cook 1 minute more, stirring. Let the mixture cool for 5 minutes.

Add the beaten eggs and cheese. Mix and spread cheese topping over the moussaka.

Bake, uncovered, for 45 minutes, then run the dish under the broiler for a few minutes to brown the top. Let stand for 10 minutes before cutting and serving.   *Serves 8*

Can be frozen

□ VEAL □

Blanquette de Veau

4 carrots
1 stalk celery
2 cups water
2 cups chicken broth
2 lbs. veal shoulder, cubed
1 tablespoon minced parsley
¼ teaspoon thyme
1 bay leaf
½ teaspoon white pepper

2 teaspoons salt
1 lb. small white onions
2 tablespoons butter
½ lb. small mushrooms
3 tablespoons butter
¼ cup flour
2 egg yolks
½ cup heavy cream
2 tablespoons lemon juice

The Night Before

Preparation Time: 30 min.   *Cooking Time:* 1 hr., 10 min.

Scrape carrots and cut carrots and celery into 2-inch pieces.

Bring water and chicken broth to a boil in a heavy pot. Add carrots, celery, veal, parsley, thyme, bay leaf, pepper, and salt. Cover pan and cook over low heat for 1 hour or until veal is tender.

Peel onions. When veal has cooked for 30 minutes, add onions to pot.

Melt 2 tablespoons butter in skillet. Sauté mushrooms until lightly browned. Set aside.

After veal has cooked for 1 hour, drain it into a colander held over a bowl. Reserve 3 cups of the liquid. Discard the celery and bay leaf.

Melt the 3 tablespoons of butter in a casserole. Add the flour and cook, stirring, until smooth. Add the 3 cups of reserved liquid. Cook and stir until sauce thickens. Remove from heat.

Beat the egg yolks, cream, and lemon juice together with a wire whisk. Slowly add ¼ cup of the hot sauce to this mixture and beat well. Then slowly add egg yolk mixture to the remainder of the thickened sauce, stirring constantly. Return to heat and cook over low heat until sauce is very thick.

Add veal, onions, carrots, and mushrooms to sauce. Stir. Cool, cover, and refrigerate.

Before Serving

Preparation Time: 1 min.   *Cooking Time:* 20 to 30 min.

Reheat covered casserole over very low heat for 15 minutes.

Remove cover and heat for 5 to 15 minutes longer, stirring occasionally. Do not let the sauce boil.   *Serves 6*

Can be frozen

Stuffed Breast of Veal

If you use a larger breast of veal than specified, in addition to increasing the stuffing proportionately, you will have to add to the cooking time about another 20 minutes per pound for every pound in excess of 3½. We don't tend to use this as a company dish and this recipe is enough for 4 to 5 portions.

3 to 3½ lbs. breast of veal (with pocket)
2 teaspoons garlic salt
½ teaspoon pepper
½ teaspoon paprika
1¼ cups grated potato (about 2 large potatoes)

1 medium onion
1 egg
1 teaspoon salt
¼ teaspoon pepper
3 tablespoons flour
2 tablespoons chicken fat or vegetable oil

The Night Before

Preparation Time: 22 min.　　　　　*Cooking Time:* 1½ hrs.

Spread the garlic salt, pepper, and paprika over the top and inside the pocket of the veal breast.

Peel the potatoes and shred them at high speed in your blender. (You can use a grater if you are able to do so without adding blood and knuckle to the mixture; we aren't.) Drain liquid off potatoes before measuring and putting them in a bowl.

Mince onion and add it to the potatoes. Beat the egg slightly and add it and the salt, pepper, and flour to the potato mixture.

Stuff the potato mixture into the pocket of the veal and skewer or sew the open end together with a trussing needle.

Heat oven to 325°. Place fat or oil in the bottom of a roasting pan. When it is melted and hot, add the veal.

When the veal has baked for about ½ hour, pour ¼ cup water over the top. Continue to bake for a total of 1½ hours, basting with the liquid in the pan 2 or 3 times.

Cover the top of the roasting pan with aluminum foil and refrigerate.

Preparation Time: 4 min.   *Cooking Time:* 1 hr.

Heat oven to 325°.

Remove aluminum foil from top of pan and roast veal for 1 hour, basting 2 or 3 times in the course of the hour.   *Serves 4*

Veal Cordon Bleu

(Allow either 1 or 2 veal scallops per person, depending on the size of the scallops you buy and the voracity of the crew you feed.)

Large, thin veal scallops   **Flavored bread crumbs**
1 slice of prosciutto ham for   **1 egg, mixed with ½ cup milk,**
    each scallop   **for each 5 or 6 scallops**
1 slice of mozzarella cheese

. . . .

Salad oil for frying

The Night Before
Preparation Time: 15 to 20 min.

On half of each veal scallop, place 1 slice of ham and 1 slice of cheese. Fold scallop over, covering filling completely. Seal edges with toothpicks. Coat each scallop in the bread crumbs, then dip into the egg-milk mixture, and then in the bread crumbs again. Store in refrigerator, putting sheets of waxed paper between layers of veal scallops. (One of the advantages of making this dish in two steps is that all breaded foods tend to keep their breading intact during the cooking process if they've been refrigerated before cooking.)

Before Serving
Preparation Time: 5 min.   *Cooking Time:* 10 to 15 min.

Heat salad oil and fry scallops until golden brown—about 10 to 15 min., turning once.

Breast of Veal Stuffed with Sausage

Breast of veal lends itself to interesting treatment and dramatic presentation. This is another cold veal dish—served with an anchovy-olive dressing—and is nice for a summer menu or for buffets.

1 cup rice
3 lbs. breast of veal, with deep pocket for stuffing
1 lb. Italian sweet sausage
1 small onion, finely chopped

2 tablespoons chopped parsley
1 clove garlic, crushed
1 egg
1 tablespoon salad oil

ANCHOVY-OLIVE DRESSING

1 cup mayonnaise
6 anchovies
8 stuffed green olives

1 clove garlic
2 slices onion

The Night Before

Preparation Time: 30 min.   *Cooking Time:* 2 hrs., 15 min.

Cook rice.

Remove sausage meat from casings. Combine with rice, onion, parsley, garlic, and egg. Pack this mixture into the pocket of the breast of veal. Close the opening with skewers or trussing needle. Use paper towels to wipe surface of veal dry.

Preheat oven to 325°.

Heat oil in a large skillet (preferably one that can go from top of stove to oven). Brown veal on all sides. Remove from heat. Wrap in aluminum foil and bake for 2 hours.

While the veal is browning, prepare the dressing. Put all ingredients for the dressing into the container of an electric blender and blend until anchovies and olives are chopped.

Refrigerate veal and dressing in separate covered serving dishes.

Before Serving

Preparation Time: 4 min.

Slice veal.

Serve sauce separately.   *Serves 4*

Swiss Veal with Cream Sauce

1¼ lb. veal cut ¼ inch thick   1 tablespoon flour
1 tablespoon brandy   1 teaspoon salt
1 small onion   ¼ teaspoon white pepper
½ lb. fresh mushrooms   1 cup chicken broth
¼ cup sweet butter

. . . .

½ cup heavy sweet cream   ¼ cup sweet butter

The Night Before

Preparation Time: 20 min.   *Cooking Time:* 10 min.

Cut the veal into strips ¼ inch wide and about 2 inches long. Sprinkle with brandy. Refrigerate.

Mince the onion fine. Rinse and slice the mushrooms.

Heat the butter in a saucepan and cook the onion and mushrooms for 3 minutes. Add the flour and stir. Then add salt, pepper, and chicken broth and cook over a moderate flame for 10 minutes. Cover and refrigerate the sauce separately.

Before Serving

Preparation Time: 5 min.   *Cooking Time:* 10 min.

Reheat the sauce in the top of a double boiler or over a flametainer or similar pot protector. When the sauce is warm, add the cream, mix thoroughly, and allow the mixture to heat for another 5 minutes, without boiling, stirring frequently.

While the sauce is warming, melt the butter in a large skillet, add the veal, and cook until the meat is browned—about 6 to 7 minutes. Place the veal in the sauce and mix before serving.   *Serves 4*

Lake Mohegan Veal Chops

6–8 veal chops, each ¾ inch thick
5 cloves garlic
⅔ cup salad oil

4 tablespoons ketchup
2 tablespoons vinegar
½ teaspoon pepper
⅓ cup soy sauce

The Night Before

Preparation Time: 5 to 10 min.

Place all ingredients other than veal chops in a blender and blend for 20 seconds. If you have no blender, crush the garlic cloves and mix them with the other ingredients by hand. Place the blended mixture in a shallow baking pan. Put the chops in the mixture, turning a couple of times to coat well. Cover the pan with aluminum foil and place in refrigerator. Turn the chops over once after a few hours or the next morning.

Before Serving

Preparation Time: 5 min.   *Cooking Time:* 20 to 25 min.

Remove chops from sauce. You have a choice of cooking method. Our personal order of preference is as follows:

Grill over charcoal for 15 to 20 min., turning once.

or

Heat electric frying pan to 350°. Cook chops for 20 min., turning once.

or

Put chops in broiler and broil for 15 min., turning once.

or

Cook over medium-high heat in an ungreased skillet for about 10 min. on each side.

(This method is fourth on the list because it's hard to cook more than a few chops at a time in a nonelectric skillet and you may have to juggle two skillets if you're feeding more than two people. A large electric skillet can take all the chops at once.)   *Serves 4*

Italian Veal with Tuna Sauce

This dish is tailor-made for the night-before cook. In fact, it can't be made by any other kind. The veal *must* be cooked the night before, refrigerated overnight, and served cold. True gourmets insist that it should be served with cold rice. If your crew balks at that notion, go ahead and use hot rice or buttered noodles. We won't tell on you!

Just one hint: If you're going to double or treble the recipe to use it for company, have your butcher make a separate roll of each 2 lbs. of veal. If you have more than 2 lbs. in a single roll, it's going to throw the cooking time off considerably.

2 lbs. boneless leg of veal, rolled and tied
1 small can (3 oz.) tuna fish
6 or 7 rolled anchovy filets, quartered
1 small onion, chopped
1½ cups dry white wine
1 tablespoon salt
¼ teaspoon pepper
¼ cup olive oil
3 tablespoons lemon juice
3 tablespoons chopped sour pickle

The Night Before

Preparation Time: 12 min.   *Cooking Time:* 1¾ hrs.

Place the meat in a heavy saucepan with the onion, anchovies, tuna, wine, salt, and pepper. Cover and simmer over low flame for 1¾ hrs.

Remove the meat to a casserole. Blend the sauce in an electric blender. (If you don't have one, put the sauce through a fine sieve twice.) Then stir in the olive oil, lemon juice, and chopped pickle. Pour the sauce over the meat. Cover the casserole and refrigerate it.

Before Serving

Preparation Time: 5 min.

Remove the meat from the sauce and slice thinly. The sauce can be served directly from the casserole in which it was stored.   *Serves 5 to 6*

Veal Ragout

Sometimes giving a recipe to a friend can prove to be a case of casting your bread on the water and having it come back with jam. This recipe was lost until a friend casually mentioned that she had served an excellent company dinner using the recipe one of us had given her 20 years earlier. She had improved it in the meantime by substituting frozen pea pods for the string beans originally specified.

1½ lbs. veal (shoulder or rump) cut ¼ inch thick
1 large onion
2 tablespoons butter
¼ lb. fresh mushrooms
⅔ of a small can of tomato paste
1 cup water

¼ teaspoon marjoram
¼ teaspoon allspice
¼ teaspoon sugar
2 teaspoons salt
1½ tablespoons flour
1 package frozen pea pods, thawed

The Night Before

Preparation and Cooking Time: 17 min.

Cut the veal into pieces about 3 inches square. Peel and slice the onion.

Melt the butter in a fairly large pan and sauté the veal and onion for about 7 minutes until the onion is soft and the veal browned lightly.

While the meat is browning, wash and slice the mushrooms.

In a bowl, mix together the tomato paste, water, marjoram, allspice, sugar, and salt.

When the veal is browned, add the flour and mix well. Pour the sauce over the meat and add the mushrooms. Mix, cover, and refrigerate.

Pat the pea pods dry between layers of paper towel and refrigerate them separately in a plastic bag or covered dish.

Before Serving

Preparation Time: 2 min.   *Cooking Time:* 1 hr.

Cook veal, covered, over a moderate flame for 1 hour.

Five minutes before the veal is finished, add the pea pods and stir.

Serves 4

Veal Soubise

The outstanding feature of this veal roast is its beautiful texture, achieved by cooking it in a covered pot, rather than an open roasting pan. An electric skillet is perfect for this recipe; it provides accurate, even heat and also makes this a one-pot operation. You may, of course, use instead a deep, heavy pot and your trusty old stove burners. As you must know by now, we are appliance addicts and prefer the electric skillet.

3 lbs. boneless veal roast, rolled and tied
2 tablespoons salad oil
2 tablespoons butter or margarine
2 large onions, sliced

Small bay leaf, or ½ large bay leaf
2 tablespoons parsley
¼ teaspoon thyme
¼ teaspoon salt
¼ teaspoon black pepper

The Night Before

Preparation Time: 20 min.   *Cooking Time:* 1½ hrs.

Heat butter and oil in skillet and brown veal on all sides—takes about 12 min. Remove veal, lower heat, and add onions, bay leaf, parsley, and thyme to skillet. Cover and cook just until onions are softened and gold-colored. Rub browned veal with salt and pepper and place in skillet (or in pot on top of stove). Set electric skillet heat control to "simmer," or simmer on top of stove over medium low flame, and cook for 1½ hrs. Remove from heat. Discard bay leaf.

Pour sauce—including the onions—into the container of an electric blender and blend until sauce is smooth. If you do not have a blender, mash onions through a sieve and stir into the sauce. Return veal and sauce to pan, cover, and refrigerate.

Before Serving

Preparation Time: 5 min.   *Cooking Time:* 20 min.

Heat both veal and sauce slowly for 20 min. Slice veal, pour sauce into gravy boat, and serve.   *Serves 6*

Veal Paprikash and Noodles

2 lbs. veal shoulder, cut in 1-inch cubes	1 clove garlic, minced
2 teaspoons salt	2 lbs. canned tomatoes
2 tablespoons flour	2 teaspoons sugar
2 tablespoons paprika	1 bay leaf
2 tablespoons salad oil	8 oz. package noodles
	1 tablespoon butter

. . . .

½ teaspoon caraway seeds   1 cup sour cream

The Night Before

Preparation Time: 30 min.   *Cooking Time:* 35 to 40 min.

Heat the oil in a 4-quart casserole, add the garlic, and cook for about 5 min. over low heat. Meanwhile, put flour, salt, and paprika into a paper bag and shake the veal cubes in this mixture until well coated. Brown the meat in the oil on all sides, using moderate heat. When well browned, add to the veal cubes the tomatoes, sugar, and bay leaf. Cover and simmer until veal is tender—about 35 min.

While the veal is browning, cook noodles according to package directions. Melt butter. Drain noodles and toss with butter. Set aside.

When veal is done, place noodles on top of meat in casserole. (Do *not* mix the noodles with the sauce.) Cover the casserole and refrigerate.

Before Serving

Preparation Time: 5 min.   *Cooking Time:* 1 hr., 5 min.

Place covered casserole in a cold oven, still leaving the noodles on top of meat. Set oven for 400° and bake for 1 hr. Stir in caraway seeds and sour cream, and *now* the noodles may be mixed with the rest of the casserole. Bake, uncovered, just until the sour cream heats through—about 5 min.

Serves 5 to 6

Veal Chops Pizzaiola

You can also make this dish with veal scallopini if you wish, using 2 scallops per person and, of course, reducing the cooking time on the meat to about 5 minutes. The sauce is excellent on beef too if you have a yen to serve a steak Italian style some night.

4 tomatoes	2 cloves garlic, minced
2 green peppers	2 teaspoons oregano
6 tablespoons parsley, minced	1 tablespoon salt
1 tablespoon olive oil	½ teaspoon pepper
. . . .	. . . . . .
6 to 8 veal chops	3 tablespoons butter

The Night Before

Preparation Time: 15 min.   *Cooking Time:* 20 min.

Drop tomatoes into boiling water for a half a minute. Remove, rinse under cold running water, peel, and dice.

Wash and stem green peppers and cut them into julienne strips. Mince garlic and parsley.

Heat oil in a pan and cook minced garlic for a minute or two, just until it is light brown. Add all the above-the-line ingredients and simmer for 20 minutes. Cover and refrigerate.

Before Serving

Preparation Time: 3 min.   *Cooking Time:* 30 min.

Sauté the chops in butter for 15 minutes on each side (350° in an electric skillet).

While the chops are browning, reheat the sauce. About 5 minutes before the chops are finished, pour the sauce over the top of the meat and cover the skillet for the last few minutes of cooking.   *Serves 4*

Anchovy Stuffed Veal Scallopini

8 veal scallops, cut thin
1 can (2-oz.) anchovy fillets
6 tablespoons whipped butter
flour

1 egg beaten with 1 tablespoon
   milk
unseasoned bread crumbs

. . . .

butter

The Night Before
Preparation Time: 12 min.

Let butter stand at room temperature until it is very soft.

Drain and chop anchovy fillets fine. Mix them well with the soft butter.

Spread the anchovy-butter mixture over one side of each veal scallop. Fold it in half with the buttered side inside.

Dip each scallop into the flour, then into the egg and milk mixture, then into the bread crumbs.

Put the breaded scallops on a platter with layers of waxed paper or plastic wrap in between layers of scallops. Cover platter and refrigerate.

Before Serving
Preparation Time: 2 min.   *Cooking Time:* 10 min.

Melt butter in a large skillet (350° if you're using an electric skillet).

Sauté scallops for 5 minutes; turn and sauté for another 5 minutes.   *Serves 4*

Veal Marinara

1 cup canned Italian tomatoes
½ cup olive oil
2 cloves garlic
1 teaspoon oregano

1 tablespoon chopped parsley
¼ teaspoon salt
Dash of pepper

. . . .

2 lbs. veal cutlet, cut ¼ inch thick
3 tablespoons butter

Salt
Pepper

The Night Before

Preparation Time: 5 min.   *Cooking Time:* 30 min.

Put all the ingredients in the blender. Run it very briefly—about 15 seconds. (If you have no blender, put the tomatoes through a sieve and crush the garlic before mixing with the other ingredients.) Pour sauce into a saucepan. Cover and simmer gently for half an hour, stirring occasionally. Cool slightly and refrigerate.

Before Serving

Preparation Time: 5 min.   *Cooking Time:* 16 min.

Melt butter in a large skillet (set at 275° if you're using an electric pan). Sprinkle the veal with a little salt and very little pepper. Sauté for about 3 min. on each side. While the veal is being sautéed, warm the sauce slightly. Pour the sauce over the veal and reduce the heat a bit (to 200° if using an electric pan). Cover and cook for 10 min., turning veal once after about 5 min.   *Serves 4*

Veal Patties with Dill Sauce

The secret of these wonderfully light, delicate patties is not cream, milk, eggs or any of the other ingredients you're likely to guess. It's club soda! If that sounds eccentric, go ahead and be eccentric; the results are worth it. The dill sauce is optional but very, very good.

VEAL PATTIES

1 onion, diced	1 cup club soda
1 tablespoon butter	1 tablespoon snipped fresh dill
1 egg	1 teaspoon salt
1¼ lbs. veal, ground twice	¼ teaspoon pepper
3 tablespoons flour	

. . . .

3 tablespoons butter

The Night Before
Preparation and Cooking Time: 18 min.

Dice the onion and sauté for about 5 minutes in the tablespoon of butter, just until it is wilted but not brown.

Beat the egg in a cup. Snip the dill with a scissors or sharp knife.

Mix the sautéed onion and the veal in a large bowl. Using a large wooden spoon, mix the flour thoroughly into the meat. Add the club soda, a little at a time, beating after each addition. Mix in the beaten egg, then the dill, salt, and pepper.

Form the meat mixture into 8 to 10 patties. (They will be soft and slippery but don't let that worry you; they'll firm up a bit in the refrigerator.) Place the patties on a flat dish, cover with plastic wrap or aluminum foil, and refrigerate.

Before Serving
Preparation Time: 2 min.   *Cooking Time:* 10 min.

Melt butter in a large skillet (350° if electric). Cook the patties for 5 minutes on each side.

If you're serving with dill sauce, heat the sauce while the patties are cooking.

DILL SAUCE

1 tablespoon butter	¼ teaspoon garlic salt
2 tablespoons flour	⅛ teaspoon onion juice
¾ cup chicken broth	2 tablespoons snipped dill
1 teaspoon Bovril beef extract	

. . . .

¾ cup sour cream

The Night Before

Preparation and Cooking Time: 8 min.

Melt butter in a saucepan. Remove from flame and stir in flour.

Return the pan to the stove and add the chicken broth gradually, stirring with a wire whisk.

Add the Bovril and stir until the sauce is smooth and thick. Add the garlic salt and onion juice and remove sauce from stove. Cool, cover, and refrigerate.

Snip the dill and refrigerate it in plastic wrap or bag.

Before Serving

Preparation and Cooking Time: 5 min.

Heat the sauce over a low flame. When it is fairly warm, add the sour cream, about a third at a time, mixing with a wire whisk. Heat to boiling point, but remove it from the stove before it actually boils.

Add the snipped dill, mix, and serve in a gravy boat.

Serves 4

Creole Veal Scallops

8 veal scallops
1 egg, lightly beaten
¼ cup milk
1½ cups bread crumbs
¼ cup salad oil
1 onion, coarsely chopped

1 cup (about 3 large stalks) diced celery
1 green pepper, chopped
1 large can (2 lbs.) tomatoes
1 teaspoon salt

The Night Before

Preparation Time: 15 min.   *Cooking Time:* 1 hr., 15 min.

Mix egg with milk. Spread bread crumbs on a flat surface. Dip veal in bread crumbs, then in egg mixture, then once again in bread crumbs. Heat oil in large skillet (325° in electric skillet) or Dutch oven and brown veal scallops on both sides. When brown, add all other ingredients, lower heat, cover, and simmer for 1 hr., 15 min. Refrigerate.

Before Serving

Cooking Time: 15 to 20 min.

Place covered pot over medium-low heat, or set electric skillet at 250°, and cook for 15 or 20 min., until heated through.

Serves 4

□ PORK □

Piperade with Ham

3 tomatoes
3 onions
2 large green peppers

2 tablespoons butter
1 teaspoon salt
¼ teaspoon pepper

. . . .

2 tablespoons butter
6 eggs
1 lb. smoked ham, cut in 4
    pieces

4 trimmed slices white bread or
    4 English muffin halves

The Night Before

Preparation Time: 20 min.   *Cooking Time:* 25 min.

Heat a pan of boiling water. Drop the tomatoes in the water for half a minute, then rinse under cold water, peel, and chop into cubes.

Cut each onion in half and slice thin.

Seed the peppers and cut in julienne slices.

Heat the butter in a small saucepan and cook the onion over moderate flame for 10 minutes until soft but not brown.

Add the rest of the above-the-line ingredients. Cover and simmer for 20 minutes. Refrigerate.

Before Serving

Preparation and Cooking Time: 10 min.

Heat the ham slices under the broiler or in a skillet with a little butter.

Heat the pan of vegetables. Meanwhile, beat the eggs. Toast the bread or muffin halves.

When the vegetables are hot, pour off all the liquid and add the butter to the pan. When it is melted, add the eggs and mix until the eggs are set.

Serve the piperade on toast with ham on the side.

Serves 4

Pork Saté

This dish is of Indonesian origin and so beloved of the Dutch settlers that they brought it back to Holland, where it's now considered almost as Dutch as pancakes or bean soup. Don't let its exotic origin frighten you. Perhaps because of the peanut flavor, it's most acceptable to the American palate.

The same dish can also be made using chunks of chicken or lamb. Follow the same recipe but cut down the cooking time slightly since neither of those needs to be cooked as thoroughly as pork.

1½ lbs. lean pork, cut in 1-inch cubes
1 medium onion, coarsely chopped
2 cloves garlic
¾ cup salted peanuts
1 teaspoon red pepper flakes

1 tablespoon ground coriander
1 tablespoon brown sugar
¼ cup soy sauce
2 tablespoons lemon juice
5 tablespoons butter
½ cup water

The Night Before

Preparation Time: 20 min.   Cooking Time: 10 min.

Cut and trim meat. Chop onion. Peel garlic.

Put in blender all ingredients except the meat, butter, and water. Blend well and transfer mixture to a saucepan.

Add the butter and water to the saucepan and cook, stirring, until the butter is melted and the mixture comes to a boil.

Put the meat cubes in a china or glass bowl and pour the sauce over it, turning several times. Cover and refrigerate the dish.

Before Serving

Preparation Time: 5 min.   Cooking Time: 15 min.

Heat broiler.

Thread the meat cubes onto 4 skewers. Reheat the sauce on top of the stove.

Broil the meat for 15 minutes, turning 2 or 3 times and basting it with the sauce when you turn it.

Serve the remaining sauce in a gravy boat with the meat.

Serves 4

Barbecued Pork Chops

This dish combines well with the Zucchini Casserole on page 198, since both require the same baking temperature and time.

8 pork chops	1 teaspoon salt
1½ tablespoons dry mustard	¼ teaspoon pepper
1 tablespoon Worcestershire sauce	1½ cups ketchup
	3 tablespoons olive oil
2 cloves garlic, crushed	

The Night Before
Preparation and Cooking Time: 12 min.

Heat 1 tablespoon olive oil in a large skillet (325° if you're using an electric skillet). If you have more chops than will fit into your skillet comfortably, you will either have to use two skillets simultaneously or brown the chops in two shifts, increasing your in-kitchen time slightly. Brown chops for 4 to 5 min. on each side.

While the chops are browning, make a paste of the mustard and Worcestershire sauce; mix with all the other ingredients, including the remaining 2 tablespoons olive oil. Remove chops from the skillet and place in a shallow oven-to-table roasting pan or wide casserole. Pour sauce over chops. Cover and refrigerate.

Before Serving
Preparation Time: 1 min. *Cooking Time: 45 min.*

Heat oven to 350°. Bake chops, covered, for 30 min. Uncover and bake for 15 min. longer.

Serves 4

Tropikabobs

2 to 2½ lbs. "ready-to-eat" (smoked or pre-cooked) ham, cut in 1½-inch cubes

1 can (11 to 12 oz.) mandarin oranges

1 can (13½ oz.) pineapple chunks

¼ cup pineapple juice from canned pineapple chunks

2 tablespoons lemon juice

8 tablespoons (1 stick) butter, or 4 tablespoons butter and 4 tablespoons margarine

3 tablespoons light brown sugar

¼ teaspoon dry mustard

2 whole cloves

The Night Before

Preparation and Cooking Time: 13 min.

Drain pineapple and oranges, reserving ¼ cup pineapple juice.

Melt butter in small, heavy saucepan. Add lemon juice, pineapple juice, sugar, mustard, and cloves. Cook together gently for 3 min. Cover saucepan and refrigerate.

Thread ham cubes, pineapple chunks, and orange sections alternately on 4 or 5 twelve-inch skewers. Leave last half inch of each skewer unfilled. Suspend the skewers across the top of a shallow baking dish. If you haven't used all the pineapple chunks or orange sections, place the rest in the bottom of the baking dish. Cover with foil or plastic wrap and refrigerate.

Before Serving

Preparation Time: 4 min.   *Cooking Time:* 8 to 10 min.

Preheat broiler. Heat sauce, which will have solidified while in the refrigerator, until it melts—this will take only a minute or two. Put baking dish, with filled skewers suspended across the top, on bottom level of broiler. Baste with half of sauce.

Broil 4 to 5 min. Turn, baste with rest of sauce, and broil for 4 to 5 min. longer.

Place skewers on serving platter and spoon sauce that has dripped into the baking dish over them. Its's nice, incidentally, if the serving platter has a bed of boiled white rice on it.

Sausage Stuffed Peppers

4 firm green peppers
4 hot Italian sausages
1 onion
1 clove garlic
⅓ cup minced parsley
2 cups beef bouillon
1 tablespoon ketchup

1 teaspoon salt
¼ teaspoon pepper
¾ cup uncooked rice
¼ cup grated Parmesan cheese
6 oz. mozzarella cheese
2 tablespoons butter

The Night Before

Preparation Time: 22 min.   *Cooking Time:* 25 min.

Boil a pot of water. Meanwhile, stem and seed the peppers. Drop them in the boiling water and cook for 4 minutes. Remove from water and allow to cool.

Remove sausages from the casings and cook the sausage meat in a saucepan over a low flame, stirring occasionally.

Mince the onion and garlic and add them to the sausage. Cook for about 10 minutes, stirring frequently until the meat is browned.

While the sausage mixture is cooking, mince the parsley. Stir the ketchup, salt, and pepper into the beef bouillon.

When the meat has browned and the onion and garlic are tender, pour off all the fat from the pan and add the rice and the bouillon mixture. Mix, bring to a boil, then cover the pan, reduce the heat, and simmer for 25 minutes. Dice the mozzarella.

Add the parsley and Parmesan cheese to the sausage-rice mixture and mix thoroughly. Stuff the mixture into the peppers and top with the diced mozzarella. Dot tops with bits of butter.

Place peppers in a baking dish, cover and refrigerate.

Before Serving

Preparation Time: 1 min.   *Cooking Time:* 35 min.

Heat oven to 350°. Bake peppers, uncovered, for 35 minutes.

Serves 4

Can be frozen before adding cheese topping

Sweet and Pungent Spareribs

3½ to 4 lbs. spareribs
2 teaspoons salad oil
½ teaspoon salt
1 clove garlic
1 green pepper, cut in 1-inch chunks
1 can (13 oz.) pineapple chunks

1½ tablespoons cornstarch
3 tablespoons sugar
¾ cup cold water
6 tablespoons red wine vinegar
1 teaspoon soy sauce
¼ cup maraschino cherries

The Night Before

Preparation Time: 25 min.

Cooking Time: 1¼ hrs. (including preparation time)

Cut meat into serving pieces (or, better still, have the butcher do it for you). Heat oven to 325°. Place meat on rack in uncovered roasting pan and bake for 1¼ hrs. Remove meat to a plate. Remove rack and drain all fat out of the pan. Replace meat in pan without rack. Cool slightly, cover with foil and refrigerate.

While the spareribs are baking, prepare sauce as follows: Heat the oil in a saucepan. Add the peeled clove of garlic and the salt and cook slowly for 10 min. Meanwhile, cut the peppers into chunks. Remove the garlic and discard it. Add to the heated oil all the syrup from the can of pineapple and the green pepper. Cook for 10 min. Meanwhile, blend the water with the cornstarch, sugar, vinegar, and soy sauce. Add this mixture to the sauce. Cook, stirring frequently, for about 5 min., until the sauce is thickened and translucent.

Add the pineapple chunks and cherries. Remove from stove, cool slightly, and store in the covered saucepan in the refrigerator.

Before Serving

Preparation Time: 5 min.

Cooking Time: 25 min.

Heat oven to 325° and place pan containing spareribs in oven. Bake for 5 min. During this time, reheat the sauce, stirring occasionally. When ribs have baked for 5 min., pour sauce over ribs and bake 20 min. longer.

This is excellent served with hot rice.   *Serves 4*

Real Fine Hambake

This is a nice touch for the ready-to-eat ham steaks or smoked ham slices you buy in the supermarket, or for just plain old leftover ham.

2 lbs. smoked or cooked ham steaks or slices (¼ inch thick)
2 tablespoons butter
2 tablespoons salad oil
2 onions, diced

2 green peppers, diced
2 cloves garlic, crushed
1 large can (3 cups) tomatoes, with their liquid
¼ teaspoon oregano

The Night Before
Preparation and Cooking Time: 25 min.

Heat butter and oil in a large skillet. Brown ham slices lightly, remove from skillet, and place side by side in a baking dish. Set aside.

Add the chopped onions to the fat remaining in the skillet, cover, and cook over low heat for 4 or 5 min. Add the sliced peppers and crushed garlic, cover, and cook over very low heat for another 5 or 6 min. Add the tomatoes and liquid and the oregano. Boil rapidly (uncovered) until most of the liquid has boiled down.

Spread the onion-pepper-tomato mixture over the ham slices. Cover and refrigerate.

Before Serving
Preparation Time: ½ min.   *Cooking Time: 20 min.*

Bake, uncovered, in a 350° oven for 20 min.   *Serves 4*

Pork and Sauerkraut Goulash

You can, if you prefer, serve this good Hungarian dish with noodles instead of potatoes. We lean toward the potatoes because we like the original menu as Miriam Brumer gave it to us: adding the potatoes to the pot in the last step and serving the goulash with "apple sauce on the side, steins of beer, and black pumpernickel bread with butter." Hard to beat as a welcome for a wintery dinner.

2 lbs. boneless fresh pork	1 teaspoon salt
2 large onions	½ teaspoon pepper
3 tablespoons cooking oil or bacon fat	2 tablespoons caraway seeds
	3 cups water
1 tablespoon vinegar	1 tablespoon tomato paste
2½ tablespoons sweet Hungarian paprika	2½ lbs. sauerkraut
	3 potatoes

. . . .

½ cup heavy sweet cream   or 1 cup sour cream

The Night Before

Preparation Time: 20 min.   *Cooking Time:* 1¾ hrs.

Cut the pork into cubes.

Slice the onions thinly. Heat the oil or bacon fat and sauté the onions until they are barely golden but not brown.

Sprinkle the vinegar and paprika over the onions and mix well. Add the pork, salt, pepper, caraway seeds, water, and tomato paste to the pot and stir well. Cover the pot and simmer for 1 hour.

Drain the sauerkraut and add it to the meat. Stir well, re-cover pot, and simmer for 45 minutes. Refrigerate.

While the meat is cooking, peel the potatoes, cut them in quarters and drop them into boiling water for 15 minutes. Drain and refrigerate in the pot in which they were cooked.

Before Serving

Preparation Time: 3 min.   *Cooking Time:* 15 min.

Heat the meat over a moderate flame. When it is slightly

warm, add the cream and mix well. Then add the potatoes to the goulash and re-cover the pot.

Cook for 15 minutes, stirring occasionally. *Serves 6*

Sausage in French Roll Crust

¾ lb. sausage meat
¼ lb. ground round steak
1 medium onion, chopped
2 tablespoons butter
½ teaspoon salt
½ teaspoon marjoram

⅓ cup water
1 egg
2 teaspoons mustard
2 brown-and-serve French rolls
    (about 8 inches long)

. . . .

2 additional tablespoons butter   1 clove garlic, crushed

The Night Before

Preparation Time: 25 min.

Sauté chopped onion in 2 tablespoons butter. Add sausage meat and cook gently for 5 to 10 min., mashing it with a fork as it cooks.

Add ground round steak and cook until browned.

Cut the ends from the brown and serve rolls. Gently hollow out the rolls, leaving the thinnest possible shell, and break the bread into soft crumbs. Add crumbs to the meat mixture. Add the egg, salt, marjoram, mustard, and water. Cover and refrigerate in the pan in which it was cooked. Refrigerate shells of French rolls.

Before Serving

Preparation Time: 10 min.   *Cooking Time:* 10 to 12 min.

Heat oven to 400°. While oven is heating, melt 2 tablespoons butter and add crushed garlic. Simmer gently for 2 min., remove from flame and set aside. Briefly reheat meat mixture over medium flame. Stuff French roll shells with meat mixture, brush with melted butter and bake for 10 to 12 min., until crusts are lightly browned. Slice and serve. *Serves 4*

Pork with Bean Sprouts

1 lb. lean pork	1 teaspoon sugar
3 slices of fresh gingerroot (see page 36)	2 scallions
	1 lb. bean sprouts, fresh or canned
¼ cup soy sauce	
2 tablespoons sherry	

. . . .

3 tablespoons peanut oil	2 tablespoons soy sauce
1½ teaspoons salt	

The Night Before

Preparation Time: 15 min.

Cut pork into ⅛-inch slices and then cut each slice into strips about ¼ inch wide by 2 to 3 inches long. (Meat is sliced more easily if left in the freezer for an hour before slicing.)

Mince ginger and mix the ginger with the soy sauce, sherry, and sugar. Put the pork in a bowl and pour the sauce over it, mixing well. Cover and refrigerate.

Mince scallions (including green part) and refrigerate separately.

Rinse bean sprouts well (even if you're using canned ones) and place between thick layers of paper towel to dry. Refrigerate in a plastic bag.

Before Serving

Preparation and Cooking Time: 7 min.

Heat 1½ tablespoons oil in a skillet or wok (350° if electric). Remove the pork, scallions, and bean sprouts from the refrigerator and place them and the salt and soy sauce near your pan.

When oil is heated, brown pork for 2 to 3 minutes, stirring frequently, until all pork strips are browned. Remove meat from pan to a separate bowl.

Add the remaining 1½ tablespoons of oil to the pan, add scallions and cook for half a minute, then add the salt and bean sprouts. Cook, stirring, for 1 minute and then add the remaining 2 tablespoons of soy sauce.

Return the pork to the pan and mix just until the meat is reheated.

Serves 4
Can be frozen

Canadian Bacon Roast

If you find yourself in the mood for a baked ham when you're not expecting company and you hesitate to make one because you don't want to eat leftover ham for days on end, this little roast is a fine substitute.

1 tablespoon lemon juice	1 cup mixed pineapple and
1 tablespoon prepared mustard	orange juice
½ cup brown sugar	1½ lbs. Canadian bacon (in 1
1 small can crushed pineapple	piece)

The Night Before
Preparation Time: 5 min.

Mix lemon juice and mustard. Add sugar and pineapple. Add enough orange juice to the pineapple juice from the can to make 1 cup and then add the juice to the sauce mixture. Cover and refrigerate.

Score tops and sides of bacon with a sharp knife. Cover and refrigerate.

Before Serving
Preparation Time: 10 min.   *Cooking Time:* 1 hr., 15 min.

Heat oven to 350°. Remove sauce from refrigerator, mix and heat slightly just to blend ingredients.

Place bacon in a small roasting pan and pour sauce over it.
Bake for 1 hour and 15 minutes, basting 3 or 4 times.

Serves 4 or 5

Apricot Pork Chops

8 pork chops
1 tablespoon olive oil
Salt
Pepper
2 tablespoons wine vinegar

1 large can (1 lb., 14 oz.) pitted apricot halves
2 tablespoons pine nuts or slivered almonds

The Night Before
Preparation and Cooking Time: 12 min.

Heat the olive oil in a large skillet (or two skillets if the chops won't all fit in one), setting the skillet at 325° if you're using an electric one. Brown the chops for 4 to 5 min. on each side.

While the chops are browning, mix the apricot halves and their juice, the vinegar, and the nuts.

When the chops have browned, sprinkle them lightly with salt and pepper. Place them in a shallow oven-to-table roasting pan and pour the fruit sauce over the chops. Cover and refrigerate.

Before Serving
Preparation Time: 1 min.   *Cooking Time: 45 min.*

Heat oven to 350°. Bake chops, covered, for 30 min. Uncover and bake for 15 min. longer.   *Serves 4*

Cranberry Ham Slice

¾ cup granulated sugar
¾ cup brown sugar
1½ tablespoons dry mustard
½ cup cider vinegar

4 tablespoons butter
1 small (8 oz.) can whole cranberry sauce

. . . .

Pre-cooked ham slice, 1 inch thick (about 2 lbs.)

The Night Before
Preparation Time: 5 min.   *Cooking Time: 10 min.*

Mix the granulated and brown sugar and mustard in a small

saucepan. Add vinegar and butter and stir. Simmer for 8 min., stirring occasionally. Add cranberry sauce and continue cooking for 2 min., stirring 3 or 4 times. Let mixture cool. Cover and refrigerate.

Before Serving

Preparation Time: 2 min.   *Cooking Time:* 15 min.

While your oven is heating to 350°, place the pan of sauce on the stove to warm slightly. Place the ham slice in a baking dish and pour sauce over it. Bake, uncovered, for 15 min.

Serves 4

Burgundy Pork Chops

8 lean pork chops	1 tablespoon brown sugar
¼ cup flour	1 tablespoon cornstarch
1 teaspoon salt	1 cup Burgundy
2 tablespoons salad oil	1 cup crushed pineapple
2 tablespoons prepared mustard	

The Night Before
Preparation and Cooking Time: 25 min.

Mix flour and salt in a paper bag. Drop pork chops in and shake vigorously until chops are coated with flour. Heat fat and brown chops until light brown. Place the chops in a casserole and place covered casserole in refrigerator.

While the chops are browning, blend the mustard, sugar, and cornstarch in a small saucepan. Add the wine and pineapple and cook, stirring until it reaches the boiling point. Cool slightly and store, in the covered saucepan, in the refrigerator.

Before Serving

Preparation Time: 2 min.   *Cooking Time:* 1 hr.

Heat oven to 350°. Heat saucepan of sauce. When hot, pour over the pork chops and place the pork chop casserole, uncovered, in the oven for 1 hr.   *Serves 4*

Scandinavian Pork Loin

Because of its long cooking time, a pork loin isn't normally a dish you might think of cooking unless you had the day off. We've found, however, that it can be cooked in two stages without a bit of harm. We think you'll find that this is a dish you can handle for a working-day meal.

If you have a talented, patient butcher, ask him to bone the loin and make a deep pocket in it. If this isn't possible, buy the loin, boned, and cut almost all the way through the middle so that you have 2 layers between which you'll place the stuffing.

4 lbs. boned pork loin	1 teaspoon salt
12 pitted prunes	½ teaspoon pepper
2 apples	2 tablespoons flour
1 medium onion	2 cups dry red wine
1½ teaspoons powdered ginger	3 tablespoons currant jelly

The Night Before

Preparation Time: 32 min.   *Cooking Time:* 1 hr., 40 min.

Split pork loin if necessary. (See note above.)

Cut prunes in half. Peel and dice apples and chop onion. Put all in a bowl and mix together with the ginger, salt, and pepper.

Heat oven to 350°.

If the butcher has made a pocket in the loin, force the stuffing into the pocket. If you've had to cut the loin in half, put the stuffing between the halves and tie the loin together with heavy butcher string at 2-inch intervals.

Place loin on a rack in a roasting pan and bake for 1½ hours. Remove the pork to a platter, cover it with aluminum foil, and refrigerate it.

Before discarding the roasting pan drippings, remove 2 tablespoons of drippings to a saucepan. Heat, add the 2 tablespoons of flour and mix well. Add the wine gradually, then the currant jelly. Cook over a medium flame for 10 minutes, stirring occasionally. Cover and refrigerate.

Before Serving

Preparation Time: 5 min.   *Cooking Time:* 1 hr.

Heat oven to 350°.

You can finish the cooking of the loin by replacing it, uncovered, on the rack of a roasting pan or by placing it into a casserole with a little of the wine sauce. We prefer the first method but if you have other things for which you need the oven space, the casserole method may be more practical. Bake on the rack or in a covered casserole for 1 hour.

A few minutes before serving time, remove the wine sauce from the refrigerator, skim the fat off, and heat the sauce. Serve the sauce in a gravy boat.

If you've tied the loin, be sure to remove string before slicing the meat.

Serves 8
Can be frozen, sliced

□ FISH AND SHELLFISH □

A Note on the Subject of Shrimp and Inflation

This is not a hint as to how to turn one pound of shrimp into three. If you know that secret, we wish you'd share it with us. It is a bit of an explanation as to why we've changed our minds in recent years on the subject of buying your shrimp already shelled and deveined.

There was a time when we preferred to avoid the time-consuming and messy job of removing those loathesome, evasive little black veins. (We both have blots on our academic escutcheons stemming from our inability to dissect anything smaller than a horse in a biology lab.) As a result, we normally tried to buy cleaned shrimp. The price differential was at one time not great when you took into account the fact that when you buy raw shrimp, you're paying for a lot of shells which you're going to discard. Partly because of the increased labor cost, the price differential is now very great. As a result, we now start with raw shrimp except in emergencies.

We have not counted the time for shelling and deveining the shrimp in the preparation time for these recipes. If you use the usual standard-size shrimp, which run about 34 to the pound, it will take you about 13 to 15 minutes to shell a pound. (Larger shrimp usually cost more, but a pound can be shelled and deveined in less time.) If you're buying your shrimp already shelled, about 12 ounces will give the same yield as 1 pound of shrimp in the shell.

Sweet and Sour Shrimp

The preparation and cooking time for this dish is a combined half hour. You will have to stay in or near the kitchen for most of that time to stir or to add ingredients. You won't be kept busy much of the time, however, and you'll have ample opportunity to prepare a molded salad or a vegetable in between working on the shrimp sauce. We like a gelatin salad and rice with this dish.

1 tablespoon salad oil	1 clove garlic
½ teaspoon salt	2 tablespoons cornstarch
3 carrots, cut in thin diagonal slices	1½ teaspoons soy sauce
	2 tablespoons sugar
2 green peppers, cut in cubes	⅓ cup red wine vinegar
1 can (13½ oz.) pineapple chunks	1¼ cups water

. . . .

1 lb. cooked, cleaned shrimp (Buy 1¾ lbs. if you buy your shrimp in the shell. See page 96.)

The Night Before
Preparation and Cooking Time: 30 min.

Heat the salad oil in a stove-to-table casserole. Add the salt and the peeled clove of garlic and simmer slowly for 5 min., stirring occasionally. Meanwhile, pare and slice the carrots and wash and dice the green peppers. When the garlic has cooked for 5 min., remove it and add to the oil the liquid from the can of pineapple and the carrots. Cook for 5 min., stirring occasionally. Then add the green peppers. Simmer for 10 min. Meanwhile, combine the cornstarch, soy sauce, sugar, and red wine vinegar. When the sauce has cooked for 10 min. after the addition of the green peppers, add the cornstarch mixture slowly, stirring well. Add the water and continue cooking, stirring, until sauce is thick—about 2 to 3 min. Remove from stove, add pineapple chunks, cool, cover, and refrigerate.

Before Serving
Preparation Time: 3 min.   *Cooking Time: 10 min.*

Add the shrimp to the sauce and simmer over a low flame for about 10 min., until mixture is warmed through. You have to watch the heat at this point, so that the sauce doesn't scorch. You can save yourself some watching and stirring time if you warm the casserole with an insulating pad over your burner.   *Serves 4*

Spicy Shrimp Dinner

4 slices bacon
3 tablespoons olive oil
1 large onion, finely chopped
½ cup celery, diced
1 clove garlic, chopped
1 tablespoon flour
1 green pepper, diced
1 can (1 lb.) tomatoes
¼ cup tomato juice
¼ cup finely chopped parsley

1 tablespoon vinegar
1 tablespoon sugar
2 tablespoons chili powder
¼ teaspoon thyme
1 teaspoon Worcestershire
    sauce
1 teaspoon horseradish
1 tablespoon lemon juice
½ teaspoon dry mustard

. . . .

1½ lbs. cooked, cleaned shrimp
    (buy 2¾ lbs. if you're buy-
    ing them with shells)

1 can (1 lb.) okra or peas
1 can (3 oz.) whole mushrooms

The Night Before

Preparation Time: 20 min.   *Cooking Time:* 35 min.

Chop the onion, garlic, and celery. Cook the bacon until crisp, but do not discard bacon fat during the cooking process. Remove the bacon from the pan and set it aside. Add the olive oil to the bacon fat and cook the onion, celery, and garlic in the combined fats for about 5 min., until the onion is transparent. Add the flour, stir, and remove the pan from the stove. Add the crumbled bacon and all the other ingredients (except the shrimp, okra or peas, and mushrooms). Stir well and simmer over a low flame for 35 min., stirring occasionally. Cool slightly, cover, and refrigerate.

If fresh shrimp are used, shell and devein them and refrigerate separately.

Before Serving

Preparation Time: 2 min.   *Cooking Time:* 30 min.

Add the shrimp, okra or peas, and mushrooms to the sauce and cook over a low flame for 30 min. This is excellent served with boiled rice.   *Serves 6*

Fish with Black Bean Sauce

This Chinese fish dish is traditionally steamed. Since you would need a 2-layer steamer to make enough for 4 people, we've adapted it for the oven. If you can't find salted or fermented black beans in a Chinese or Japanese grocery near you, you can order them from one of the sources listed on page 12. They can be kept in a tightly covered jar on your pantry shelf for months.

3 tablespoons salted black beans
1 tablespoon finely chopped garlic

1½ tablespoons soy sauce
1½ tablespoons sherry
1½ tablespoons vegetable oil
¼ teaspoon white pepper

. . . .

1½ lbs. filet of sole or flounder

The Night Before

Preparation Time: 7 min.

Put the black beans in a strainer and rinse under running cold water.

With a sharp knife, mince the black beans and garlic together.

Mix all ingredients together in a small bowl, cover, and refrigerate.

Before Serving

Preparation Time: 2 min.   *Cooking Time:* 15 to 20 min.

Heat oven to 350°. Grease the bottom of a large baking pan lightly with oil.

Put the fish in the pan without overlapping the pieces. Pour the black bean sauce over the top. Bake for 15 to 20 minutes, depending on the thickness of the filets. The fish is done when it flakes easily with a fork.

Serves 4

Main-Dish Fish Chowder

This New England-style chowder combines two virtues not often found in one dish—it is exquisitely flavored, yet hearty enough to satisfy even the most ravenous appetites. A meal planned around this soup should contain little else—a fruit salad, some crusty French bread, and a very light, cold dessert nicely complement the chowder, making a more than ample meal.

5- or 6-oz. piece salt pork, cut into chunks
2 cups water
2 onions, coarsely chopped
3 large potatoes, diced

3 tablespoons butter
3 tablespoons flour
2 cups milk
black pepper

. . . .

1 lb. frozen cod fillets (other fish, fresh or frozen, may be used successfully)
additional milk, if necessary

The Night Before

Preparation Time: 15 min.   *Cooking Time:* 40 min.

Place the chunks of salt pork in a heavy 4-quart pot and cook over medium-high heat for 15 minutes to render part of the fat.

Meanwhile, chop the onions, and peel and dice the potatoes into rather large chunks.

Prepare this white sauce, which will be used later to thicken the chowder: melt the butter in a saucepan, stir in flour and cook until smooth; add milk, cooking and stirring until mixture thickens. Remove from heat and reserve.

Add the 2 cups water to the salt pork and melted fat. Bring to a fast boil, then simmer for 5 minutes. Add onions, cover, and simmer for 10 minutes. Add potatoes, cover, and simmer for 10 minutes more.

Stir white sauce into the soup and cook together for a minute or two. Season to taste with black pepper.

Cover and refrigerate.

Before Serving

Preparation Time: 1 min.   *Cooking Time:* 15 to 20 min.

Place frozen fish fillets on top of chowder, cover, and simmer for 15 to 20 minutes. The cooking time here depends on the type and thickness of the fish used, and on whether it is fresh or frozen. (The fish is done if it flakes easily when tested with a fork.) If the chowder seems a bit too thick for your taste, thin it with milk.

Baked Salmon Casserole

Parsley mayonnaise (page 180) goes well with this.

3 slices white bread	3 sprigs parsley
1 can (1-lb.) salmon	½ teaspoon salt
½ medium onion, sliced	¼ teaspoon dry mustard
2 eggs	⅛ teaspoon Tabasco
2 tablespoons butter	¾ cup milk
¼ cup celery leaves	

The Night Before

Preparation Time: 15 min.

Tear each slice of white bread into 6 or 7 pieces and place one slice at a time in the blender. Blend for 3 or 4 seconds and pour crumbs into a large mixing bowl before blending the next slice.

Place all the remaining ingredients in the blender and blend on high speed for about ½ minute. Pour blended mixture over bread crumbs and mix well.

Cover and refrigerate.

Before Serving

Preparation Time: 2 min.   *Cooking Time:* 50 min.

Heat oven to 375°. Butter the inside of a 1-quart casserole and pour salmon mixture into it.

Bake, uncovered, for 50 minutes.   *Serves 4*

Fish Cakes

These might well be called "fish cakes for people who don't think they like fish cakes." Between school cafeterias and the stuff purveyed by the frozen food processors, you may have become so disenchanted that you're tempted to pass this recipe by. Don't! These are delicate and delicious. They really don't need any sauce at all but if you do want one, please don't short-cut with a canned tomato sauce that will bury the beauty of your creation. Use the tomato sauce suggested right after this recipe.

1½ lbs. fish fillets (flounder or sole)	3 egg yolks
1 onion	6 tablespoons milk
¾ cup fine bread crumbs	1 teaspoon salt
¼-lb. stick of butter	¼ teaspoon white pepper

. . . .

3 to 4 tablespoons butter for frying

The Night Before

Preparation Time: 15 min.

Put fish and onion through the food grinder.

Add the bread crumbs and mix. Then add the butter in small pieces, working it into the fish mixture with your hands as you would a pastry dough.

Add all remaining ingredients and mix well. Form the mixture into 12 fish cakes. Put on a flat plate, cover with plastic wrap or aluminum foil, and refrigerate.

Before Serving

Preparation Time: 2 min.   *Cooking Time:* 10 min.

Melt butter in a skillet over a medium flame (350° if you're using an electric skillet).

Fry cakes for about 5 minutes or until golden brown on one side; turn and fry the other side for 5 minutes.

Note: The recipe can be doubled, and part of the uncooked fish cakes can be frozen for future use. They should be thawed before being fried.

Serves 4

Tomato Sauce

3 large tomatoes
1 small Bermuda onion, chopped
1 stalk celery, sliced
1 small carrot, sliced
1 clove garlic, minced

2 tablespoons olive oil
1 teaspoon salt
⅛ teaspoon pepper
¼ teaspoon basil
½ teaspoon sugar

The Night Before

Preparation Time: 12 min.　　　　　　*Cooking Time:* 45 min.

Drop the tomatoes in boiling water for 1 minute, rinse under cold water, and peel and dice them.

Chop the onion, celery, carrot, and garlic and sauté in the olive oil for about 3 to 4 minutes.

Add the diced tomatoes and all other ingredients to the sautéed vegetables and cook over a low flame for 45 minutes, stirring occasionally.

Let the sauce cool slightly, then run it through the blender. Refrigerate, covered.

Before Serving

Preparation Time: 1 min.　　　　　　*Cooking Time:* 5 min.

Heat the sauce over a low flame, stirring occasionally, until it is hot. Place sauce in a gravy boat and serve with the fish cakes.

Filet of Sole in Sherry and Cream Sauce

2 lbs. sole or flounder filets
2 scallions, chopped
2 tablespoons butter
¾ cup dry sherry (or other dry white wine, if you prefer)
¾ cup cold water
2 egg yolks
Scant ¾ cup heavy cream

3 tablespoons butter
¼ cup flour
¾ cup milk
¼ teaspoon salt
¼ teaspoon lemon juice
3 tablespoons grated Swiss cheese
Extra butter (for dotting)

The Night Before
Preparation and Cooking Time: 35 min.

Preheat oven to 350°. Butter a baking dish that can be used on top of the stove, in the oven, under the broiler, and for serving. Spread half the scallions on bottom of dish. Fold each filet in half and place filets, side by side, over scallions. Spread rest of scallions on top of filets. Dot with 2 tablespoons butter. Mix sherry and water together and pour over fish. Cook over medium heat on top of stove until liquid simmers—takes about 5 min. Remove from heat.

Place a piece of waxed paper directly on top of fish. Bake in 350° oven for 10 min. While the fish is baking, start preparing the sauce.

Beat egg yolks and ½ cup cream together in a large bowl until they are well blended. Set aside. Melt 3 tablespoons butter in a saucepan, add flour, and cook over low heat, stirring constantly, until mixture thickens and bubbles. Remove from heat.

Remove fish from oven and pour off liquid, reserving 1 cup. Add reserved liquid to butter-flour mixture. Stir vigorously, then stir in milk. Return to heat, bring to boil, and boil for 1 min., stirring all the while. Remove from heat. Add this sauce, a tablespoonful at a time, to the bowl containing the egg yolks and cream. Beat in each spoonful thoroughly (a wire whisk is helpful here) before adding the next—this will give you the smooth consistency that could not be achieved otherwise. Return the sauce to the pan and, stirring constantly, bring to boil over fairly high heat, then continue to boil for 1 min. Stir in remaining ¼ cup cream to thin sauce. Add salt and lemon juice, taste, and correct seasoning if necessary.

Pour sauce over fish. Top with grated Swiss cheese and dot with butter. Cover and refrigerate.

Before Serving

Preparation Time: 2 min.   *Cooking Time:* 12 to 14 min.

Preheat broiler. Place uncovered dish on top of stove and cook over medium heat until sauce begins to bubble. Then put under broiler, 4 inches from heat, until top of sauce browns.
Serves 4

Baked Bluefish and Bacon

You can give yourself a night-before off if you want to—this recipe takes about two minutes of preparation time.

We have specified 2-pound bluefish, but the owner of the fish market may not have read this book. If a single, larger fish is what is available, simply split it and use it (skin side down) as if it were two fish.

2 bluefish, about 2 lbs. each,   2 lemons, cut into quarters
    cleaned   few sprigs parsley
6 slices bacon

Before Serving

Preparation Time: 2 min.   *Cooking Time:* 25 min.

Heat oven to 425°.

Grease a baking dish and place fish in it. Bake for 5 minutes.

Place strips of bacon on top of fish. Bake about 20 minutes longer, until fish flakes easily when tested with a fork.

Remove fish to a platter and garnish with lemon wedges and parsley.
Serves 4

Pat's Fish Stew

This dish involves quite a lot of chopping but if you do it at the times indicated in the recipe, the total preparation time is not too horrendous. And the result is, to put it mildly, glamorous.

½ cup salad oil
1 cup flour
2 medium onions, chopped
3 stalks celery, chopped
1 small green pepper, chopped
1 clove garlic, chopped
1 small can tomato paste
1 teaspoon Worcestershire
  sauce

1 can (10 oz.) tomatoes
4 cups hot water
1½ cups parsley, chopped
3 scallions, including green
  tops, chopped
¼ lb. (1 stick) butter or margarine
4 thin slices of lemon

. . . .

1½ lbs. red snapper or pom-
  pano, boned

1½ teaspoons salt
1¼ cups Burgundy

The Night Before

Preparation Time: 35 min.   *Cooking Time:* 15 min.
                                    (in addition to preparation time)

Chop the onions, green pepper, celery, and garlic. Heat the salad oil in a very large (6 quart) casserole over a low flame. Add the flour gradually, stirring, until the mixture is thick, smooth, and a very light brown. Add onions, celery, garlic, and green pepper. Mix well. Add tomato paste, Worcestershire sauce, and tomatoes and cook for 5 min. Gradually add hot water, stirring after each addition. When all water has been added, simmer for 10 min. Meanwhile, chop the scallions and parsley.

After the mixture has simmered for 10 min., add the scallions, parsley, lemon, and butter. Stir and let simmer for 15 min. Cool and refrigerate.

Before Serving

Preparation Time: 3 min.   *Cooking Time:* 35 min.

Reheat the sauce for 5 min. Meanwhile, cut the fish into

pieces about 3 inches square. Add the fish and salt to the sauce and stir gently. Cook for 10 min.; then add the wine and let the stew simmer for 20 min. more. Remove the lemon slices before serving. (Rice goes well with this and may be prepared while the stew is simmering.) *Serves 6*

Cod Provençal

1 onion	¼ cup olive oil
2 cloves garlic	½ cup dry white wine
3 large, ripe tomatoes (if fresh ripe tomatoes are unavailable, use canned tomatoes)	¼ teaspoon freshly ground black pepper
4 anchovies	8 sprigs parsley

. . . .

1½ lbs. cod filets

The Night Before

Preparation Time: 17 min.

Chop onion. Mince garlic. Plunge tomatoes into boiling water for 30 seconds, then peel, seed, and chop tomatoes. Chop anchovies fine.

Heat olive oil in a very large skillet. Sauté onion and garlic until onion is translucent. Add chopped tomatoes and cook over low heat for 5 minutes. Add wine, raise heat, and cook for 5 minutes longer. Remove from heat. Add pepper and chopped anchovies. Cover and refrigerate.

Mince parsley and store in covered container in refrigerator.

Before Serving

Preparation Time: 1 min.   *Cooking Time:* 20 min.

Heat sauce in skillet until it begins to boil.

Lower heat and place cod filets in sauce, spooning some of the sauce over the fish. Cover and simmer for 15 minutes.

Sprinkle with minced parsley. *Serves 4*

Lobster Tails Fra Diavolo

8 lobster tails (We use frozen lobster tails, which tend to be small, and we find 2 per portion are needed. If the lobster tails you buy are large, 1 per person may be enough. If you are using frozen lobster, be sure it is thawed before you start your night-before preparation.)

¼ cup olive oil
1 clove garlic, chopped
1 can (1 lb.) plum tomatoes
¼ teaspoon crushed red pepper seeds
1¼ teaspoons oregano
½ teaspoon salt
Dash pepper

The Night Before

Preparation Time: 15 min.   *Cooking Time:* 12 min.

Heat the olive oil in a saucepan and cook the chopped garlic in the oil over a low flame for about 2 min. Add all the other ingredients except the lobster. Stir; simmer for 10 min., stirring occasionally.

While the sauce is simmering, cut through the soft cartilage of each lobster tail with a kitchen scissors and bend the edges back to expose a maximum amount of the lobster meat. Arrange the lobster tails in the baking dish in which they will be cooked. Cover the dish with aluminum foil and refrigerate.

When the sauce has cooked for 10 min., allow it to cool slightly, then cover and refrigerate it.

Before Serving

Preparation Time: 3 min.   *Cooking Time:* 25 min.

Heat oven to 350°. While it is heating, place the pan of sauce on the stove and reheat slightly. Pour the sauce over the lobster tails and bake for 25 min.   *Serves 4*

Flounder Stuffed with Shrimp

6 sprigs parsley	1½ cups frozen shrimp,
2 tablespoons butter	unthawed (or 1½ cups
2 tablespoons flour	shelled fresh shrimp)
1 cup plus 2 tablespoons milk	1½ lbs. flounder filets
1½ teaspoons dry mustard	2 slices white bread
1 teaspoon salt	

. . . .

2 tablespoons butter

The Night Before

Preparation Time: 12 min.

Mince parsley. Set aside.

Melt butter in saucepan. Add flour and stir until smooth. Add milk and cook, stirring, until sauce is thick. Add dry mustard, salt, parsley, and shrimp. Cook and stir for 5 minutes. Remove from heat.

Grease an 8" x 12" baking pan. Place a few shrimp and about 2 teaspoons of sauce on each filet. Roll filets and place in baking pan with loose edge down. Spoon remaining sauce over tops of filets. Cover and refrigerate.

Tear bread into pieces and put in electric blender to make bread crumbs. Store bread crumbs in plastic bag.

Before Serving

Preparation Time: 3 min.   *Cooking Time:* 20 min.

Heat oven to 375°.

Sprinkle bread crumbs over tops of rolled flounder filets. Dot with butter.

Bake, uncovered, for 15 minutes. Spoon pan juices over filets. Broil until tops are golden brown—about 5 minutes.

Serves 6

Baked Striped Bass with Mushroom-Onion Stuffing

1 small onion	3 lb. striped bass with backbone
1 large onion	removed to form cavity for
4 large mushrooms	stuffing
10 sprigs parsley	salt
¼ cup butter	pepper
4 slices white bread	2 tablespoons butter

. . . .

½ cup dry white wine	2 lemons

The Night Before

Preparation Time: 25 min.

Chop small onion. Slice large onion into rings. Wipe mushrooms with damp cloth; cut caps in half and slice thin; chop stems. Mince parsley.

Melt butter in a skillet and sauté mushrooms for 5 minutes. Add chopped onion and sauté until onion is golden. Remove from heat.

Prepare bread crumbs: tear each slice of white bread into several pieces and process a few pieces at a time in the electric blender. Add bread crumbs and parsley to mushrooms and onions; mix well.

Arrange the sliced onion on the bottom of a greased baking dish—the bed of onion rings should correspond roughly to the shape of the fish. Sprinkle the fish, inside and out, with salt and pepper. Stuff with bread-crumb mixture. Secure opening with skewers or sew with trussing needle and string. Place fish on onion bed. Dot with butter, cover, and refrigerate.

Before Serving

Preparation Time: 2 min.   *Cooking Time:* 35 min.

Heat oven to 400°.

Pour wine into baking dish. Squeeze juice of one lemon over and around fish. Bake, uncovered, for about 35 minutes, basting occasionally with pan juices. Fish is done when it flakes easily with a fork. Garnish with second lemon, cut into wedges.

Serves 4

Baked Shrimp

2 lbs. shrimp
¼ cup parsley, chopped
2 cloves garlic
¼ cup chives
6 tablespoons butter
2 teaspoons Worcestershire
    sauce

½ teaspoon salt
⅛ teaspoon pepper
1 tablespoon bread crumbs
3 tablespoons grated Parmesan
    cheese

The Night Before
Preparation and Cooking Time: 20 min.

Shell and devein shrimp.

Mince parsley and garlic as well as chives if you're using fresh chives.

Melt 5 tablespoons of the butter in a wide skillet or saucepan. Add the shrimp and all other ingredients except the bread crumbs, grated cheese, and the reserved tablespoon of butter.

Cook for about 5 minutes, stiring frequently, until all shrimp are pink. Turn the mixture into a one-quart casserole.

Sprinkle bread crumbs, then grated cheese over the top of the mixture. Cut the remaining tablespoon of butter in small bits and sprinkle them over the top of the shrimp.

Cover the casserole and refrigerate.

Before Serving
Preparation Time: 1 min.   *Cooking Time:* 15 min.

Preheat oven to 400°.

Bake casserole, uncovered, for 15 minutes, until cheese topping is lightly browned.

Serves 4

Crabmeat Casserole

2 cans crabmeat (8 oz. each)	2 beaten egg yolks
6 tablespoons butter	2 tablespoons sherry
6 tablespoons flour	1 cup soft bread crumbs
2 cups milk	1 tablespoon minced parsley
⅛ teaspoon pepper	1 teaspoon minced onion
½ teaspoon celery salt	

. . . .

¼ cup fine, dry bread crumbs	1 tablespoon butter
Paprika	

The Night Before

Preparation Time: 30 min.   *Cooking Time:* 10 min.

Melt the 6 tablespoons butter. Add flour and blend. Add milk, celery salt, and pepper. Cook over low heat, stirring constantly until thickened. Add egg yolks and cook 2 min. longer, stirring constantly.

Remove from stove and add sherry, soft bread crumbs, crabmeat, parsley, and onion. Mix gently and pour into greased 1½ quart casserole. Refrigerate, covered.

Before Serving

Preparation Time: 5 min.   *Cooking Time:* 40 min.

Heat oven to 400°. Sprinkle dry bread crumbs over casserole and dot with butter. Sprinkle lightly with paprika.

Bake, uncovered, for 40 min.   *Serves 4*

Filet of Sole in Parsley Sauce

¼ lb. (1 stick) butter	3 tablespoons chopped scallions
2 tablespoons lemon juice	1 teaspoon salt
3 tablespoons chopped parsley	⅛ teaspoon thyme

. . . .

2 lbs. filet of sole

The Night Before

Preparation Time: 15 min.

Cream the butter in a small, heavy saucepan. Blend in lemon juice, parsley, scallions, salt, and thyme. Cover saucepan with a tight-fitting cover or with foil and refrigerate.

Before Serving

Preparation Time: 5 min.   *Cooking Time:* 20 min.

Heat oven to 350°. While oven is heating, heat the sauce slowly on top of the stove. Pour half the heated sauce into an oven-to-table serving dish. Place the filets of sole in the dish and pour the remaining sauce over them. Bake for approximately 20 min. (Baking time will depend on the thickness of the filets. Test for doneness by flaking the fish with a fork; it is done when it flakes easily.)   *Serves 4*

Swordfish Steaks with Sherry-Soy Sauce

⅓ cup soy sauce   ½ teaspoon ginger
½ cup sherry   2 lbs. swordfish steaks, about
1 tablespoon peanut oil   ¾ inch thick
1 clove garlic

The Night Before

Preparation Time: 3 min.

Combine all ingredients except fish in container of electric blender and blend until well mixed.

Arrange swordfish steaks in greased baking dish. Pour marinade over and around fish. Cover and refrigerate. Turn the fish in the marinade later that night or in the morning.

Before Serving

Preparation Time: 2 min.   *Cooking Time:* 10 min.

Preheat broiler. Spoon marinade over top of fish.

Broil for about 5 minutes on each side, basting with marinade before broiling second side.   *Serves 4*

Salmon Vinaigrette

This salmon is served cold. We like to serve it accompanied by parsley mayonnaise (page 180).

1 lb. salmon steak, cut at least ¾ inch thick	⅛ teaspoon pepper
1 medium onion, quartered	1 bay leaf
¼ teaspoon salt	2 cups vinegar
¼ teaspoon sugar	4 cups water

The Night Before

Preparation Time: 5 min.   *Cooking Time:* 50 min.

Put all ingredients except the salmon steak into a pot and and cook over a high flame for 25 min. Heat the oven to 325°. Pour some of the liquid into the bottom of a roasting pan or a casserole which is large enough for the salmon steaks to be placed flat in it. Lay the salmon steaks gently in the liquid and pour the rest of liquid around the pieces of fish. Bake, uncovered, for 25 min. Remove from oven, cool, cover and refrigerate the dish.

Before Serving

Preparation Time: 1 min.

Carefully remove the salmon steaks from the liquid, using a spatula.   *Serves 4*

Crab and Shrimp Casserole

2 tablespoons butter	1 can (7½-oz.) crabmeat
⅓ cup unseasoned bread crumbs	1 can (4½- or 5-oz.) small shrimp
1 cup celery, diced	1 cup mayonnaise
½ large green pepper, diced	¼ teaspoon Worcestershire sauce
½ cup chopped onion	
1 cup (loosely packed) minced parsley	

The Night Before

Preparation Time: 20 min.

Melt butter and mix it with the bread crumbs.

Chop the celery, green pepper, onion, and parsley.

Mix all ingredients except the buttered bread crumbs in a bowl. Lightly butter a 1½-quart casserole and turn the mixture into the casserole. Top with the bread crumbs.

Cover casserole and refrigerate it.

Before Serving

Preparation Time: 1 min.   *Cooking Time:* 45 min.

Heat oven to 350°.

Bake casserole, uncovered, for 45 minutes.   *Serves 4*

Gefilte Fish

These traditional Jewish ground fish balls might be described as the peasant cousin of the delicate French *quenelle*. Unlike the *quenelle*, however, they can and should be made the night before so that they can be served cold.

Some people serve this as an appetizer and that's all right provided you serve only one fish ball per person and lie if necessary when asked for seconds; otherwise you might have no customers for the main course. Since we prefer to lie only in emergencies, we suggest these as the heart of a light main course. Serve it with sliced tomatoes and cucumbers and a bit of lettuce as a setting.

Have the fish market bone and skin the fish and give you the heads, bones, and skin separately. Have the boned fish ground. (If your fish market can't grind it for you, add a few minutes to the preparation time for a first grinding.)

The trick with gefilte fish is to combine a lean fish with a fat one. We've been a little skeptical about traditional formulas of how much of which fish to use since the time an elderly lady of our acquaintance got stuck at the last minute and had to run from fish store to fish store on the eve of a holiday and take whatever kind of fish happened to be left. She produced the best gefilte fish of her over seventy years of cooking and was never able to recapture it because, like the lost chord, she had no idea of what went into it!

FOR THE BROTH

6 cups water	¾ teaspoon pepper
2 onions, sliced	heads, skin, and bones of fish
1 tablespoon salt	

FOR THE FISH BALLS

4 to 4½ lbs. mixed whitefish,
    carp, and pike, boned,
    skinned, and ground
1 large onion
½ teaspoon sugar

3 tablespoons matzo meal
2 teaspoons salt
¾ teaspoon pepper
3 eggs, beaten
½ cup ice water

. . . .

red horseradish

The Night Before

Preparation Time: 32 min.   *Cooking Time:* 2 hrs., 10 min.

Combine all the broth ingredients in a large pot. Bring to a boil, then reduce heat and simmer for 40 minutes. Strain and discard everything but the broth.

Grind the fish and onion together using the coarse blade of a meat grinder. Put in a large bowl and add all other ingredients. Mix well.

Form the fish mixture into oblong patties and drop gently in the fish broth. Cover pot and simmer for 1 hour, then remove cover and simmer for an additional half hour.

Allow the fish to cool in the broth slightly before removing it to a platter for refrigeration.

Before Serving

Serve fish cold with red horseradish on the side.

Serves 12 as appetizer or
4 to 6 as main course

Clams Marinara

You can build a delightful, different summer meal around this dish—start with a good mixed salad, then clams marinara served with lots of fresh French or Italian bread for mopping up the marinara sauce, and end with fresh fruit. If there's any marinara sauce left in the pot, refrigerate or freeze it and use it as sauce for spaghetti.

4 dozen littleneck clams in shells	8 parsley sprigs
½ cup cornmeal	⅛ teaspoon black pepper
2 garlic cloves	⅛ teaspoon crushed red pepper

THE SAUCE

3 garlic cloves	1 tablespoon oregano
16 parsley sprigs	½ teaspoon salt
¼ cup olive oil	¼ teaspoon pepper
2 tablespoons butter	6 anchovy fillets
large can (2 lbs. 3 oz.) Italian tomatoes	2 tablespoons tomato paste

. . . .

3 tablespoons olive oil	¾ cup white wine
3 tablespoons butter	French or Italian bread

The Night Before

Preparation Time: 30 min.   *Cooking Time:* 35 min.

Scrub clams well with a stiff brush, rinsing under cold running water. Set them in a pot of cold water, to which you have added ½ cup cornmeal, for an hour to loosen any remaining particles of sand, then rinse again and refrigerate.

With a garlic press, crush 2 cloves and set aside with 8 parsley sprigs (without stems) and the black and red pepper in a small dish. Cover and refrigerate.

Heat the olive oil and butter in a saucepan. Crush and add the 3 remaining cloves of garlic and the 16 parsley sprigs (without stems) and cook over low heat for 5 minutes. Drain and chop the tomatoes; add tomatoes, oregano, salt, and pepper; and simmer over a low flame for ½ hour, stirring occasionally.

Add anchovies and tomato paste to sauce and mix well. Remove from heat, cool, cover, and refrigerate.

Before Serving

Preparation Time: 7 min.   *Cooking Time:* 25 min.

Add the wine to the sauce and reheat slightly.

Place the butter and olive oil in a large soup pot or Dutch oven. When butter is melted, add the clams and sprinkle the reserved parsley-garlic mixture over them. Cover and cook for 5 minutes.

Pour the sauce over the clams. Cover and cook for 15 minutes.

Note: If you like mussels enough to spend half an hour debearding them, you may successfully substitute mussels for clams in this recipe. We suggest that you hurry and do it before the price of mussels goes up—they are becoming increasingly popular and probably won't be inexpensive very much longer.   *Serves 4*

See also: Spaghetti with Oyster Sauce (page 157).

◻ FOWL ◻

Many of these recipes call for a 3 to 3½ lb. chicken. Since you will be using fairly short cooking times, it is important not to buy an emaciated stewing hen. Your safest bet is what is known as a broiler-fryer—a somewhat misleading name, since this type of young chicken takes well to many kinds of cooking other than broiling or frying.

Oriental Chicken

3½ lb. frying chicken, cut in parts	2 tablespoons molasses
½ cup honey	½ cup soy sauce
¼ cup vinegar	2 cups water

. . . .

¾ cup sifted flour	2 cups salad oil
1 tablespoon salt	

The Night Before

Preparation Time: 10 min.   *Cooking Time:* 50 min.

Place chicken and 2 cups water in a pot. Cover, bring to a boil, then reduce heat, and simmer for 45 min. Drain the chicken, rinse it in cold water, and dry with paper towels.

Make a marinade of the honey, vinegar, molasses, and soy sauce. Brush the chicken with the marinade and place the chicken in a large bowl, pouring the remaining marinade over it. Refrigerate. Turn the pieces over in the marinade once the next morning.

Before Serving

Preparation and Cooking Time: 10 min.

If you're using an electric skillet, heat it to 375°; then add the oil and allow it to heat to the same temperature. If you're still cooking without an electric skillet (and we don't quite understand why you should be at this point), heat the oil in a heavy skillet or deep fat fryer to 375°.

While the oil is heating, put the flour and salt in a paper bag; add the chicken pieces, a few at a time, and shake the bag vigorously to coat the chicken with the flour. Fry the chicken until golden brown. This will take only 2 to 3 min. Drain on paper towels. *Serves 4*

Superfast Chicken

This method of preparing chicken is so simple that it barely falls into the "recipe" category. However, so many people have asked us how it's done that we suppose it really should be included in this collection. It does taste very, very good—especially for something that takes exactly one minute of your time.

1 fryer, cut into at least 8
   pieces
seasoned salt

Before Serving

Preparation Time: 1 min.   *Cooking Time:* 30 min.

Preheat oven to 450°.

Arrange chicken pieces, skin side up, in baking pan. Sprinkle generously with seasoned salt.

Bake, uncovered, for 30 minutes. If a crisper skin is desired, place under the broiler for 2 or 3 minutes at the end of the baking period.

A rather nice variation of this can be prepared using duck sauce instead of seasoned salt—just spoon the duck sauce over the chicken before baking. The same basic method—using either seasoned salt, duck sauce, or barbecue sauce—also makes the best chicken we've ever tasted at an outdoor barbecue. The trick is to cook the chicken in the oven for 20 minutes before placing it over the charcoal fire just long enough to complete the cooking and give it an attractively crisp appearance.

Serves 4

Duck with Apricots

5 lb. duck, cut in parts	3 cloves garlic
1½ teaspoons salt	8 oz. canned apricot juice
¼ teaspoon pepper	¾ cup dried apricots

The Night Before

Preparation Time: 10 min.   *Cooking Time:* 1 hr.

Heat oven to 325°. Sprinkle duck with salt and pepper and place, skin side up, on a rack in a baking pan. Bake 1 hr.

While duck is baking, boil the apricots for 15 to 20 min. and discard water. Mash garlic and mix garlic, apricot juice, and apricots together.

When duck has baked for 1 hr., drain off all fat. Remove the rack and put duck in bottom of pan, pouring the apricot mixture over it. Cover and refrigerate.

Before Serving

Preparation Time: 1 min.   *Cooking Time:* 35 min.

Heat oven to 325°, and bake, uncovered, for 35 min. *Serves 6*

Duck à l'Orange

You can make this by using the basic recipe given above for the Duck with Apricots. Just omit the garlic, apricots, and apricot juice and, instead of the apricot sauce, make the following sauce:

2 tablespoons sugar	¾ teaspoon cornstarch
¼ cup currant jelly	2 tablespoons water
2 oz. orange juice	2 tablespoons julienne orange
2 tablespoons port	rind

Combine sugar, jelly, and juice in a saucepan. Bring to a boil and simmer over low flame for 15 minutes.

Add wine and cook 5 minutes.

Mix cornstarch and water and add to sauce, stirring until it comes to boil. Remove from heat and add orange rind.

Add the sauce to the duck at the point indicated in the previous recipe.

Spanish Chicken

1 chicken (3½ lbs.) cut in serv-
    ing pieces
¼ cup olive oil
1 cup uncooked rice
1 medium onion, chopped
1 small green pepper, chopped

2 cloves garlic, chopped
3 tomatoes, cut in quarters
1 can (8½ oz.) green peas
1 tablespoon salt
1½ cups water

The Night Before

Preparation Time: 35 min.   *Cooking Time:* 30 min.

Heat oil in a heavy skillet (350° for an electric skillet) or a heavy pot. Sauté chicken until lightly browned. Remove chicken to a platter. Sauté the rice in the same skillet or pot, stirring constantly, until rice is golden. Add the onion, garlic, and green pepper and cook, stirring frequently, for 5 min. Remove from heat and stir in the tomatoes, salt, and green peas. Place this mixture and the chicken in a casserole and pour the water over the top. It is important to be sure that the rice is covered by the water or is under the tomatoes so that it has sufficient liquid to ensure adequate cooking.

Place the casserole, covered, in a 400° oven. Bake for ½ hr. Cool and refrigerate.

Before Serving

Preparation Time: 1 min.   *Cooking Time:* 40 min.

Heat oven to 400°. Check casserole to be sure rice is still in liquid and not on top of the chicken. Add a little water if necessary. Bake, uncovered, for 40 min.   *Serves 4 to 5*

Chicken Paprikash with Dumplings

1 large onion
3 tablespoons butter
2 tablespoons Hungarian sweet
　　paprika
1 tablespoon salt
½ teaspoon pepper

3- to 3½-lb. chicken, cut in
　　pieces
2 cups water or chicken broth
2 tablespoons flour
1 cup sour cream

FOR THE DUMPLINGS

2 eggs
¼ cup water
1½ cups sifted flour

2 tablespoons parsley, finely
　　minced

The Night Before

Preparation Time: 30 min.　　　　　　*Cooking Time:* 50 min.

Dice onion and sauté it in a Dutch oven in the butter. When it is wilted but not brown, sprinkle the paprika, salt, and pepper over it, mix well and push the onions to the side of the pan.

Sauté the chicken pieces in the same pot until lightly golden on all sides.

Add the water or chicken broth, mix well, and simmer, covered, for 40 minutes.

While the chicken is cooking, heat a pan of water for the dumplings.

Beat the eggs and water together. Add flour and mix until smooth. Add parsley and mix again. Drop the dumplings by the teaspoonful into boiling water. Cover pan, reduce heat, and let simmer for 10 minutes. Drain and set dumplings aside.

When the chicken has cooked for 40 minutes, remove from heat. Take chicken out of sauce and set it aside.

Add the 2 tablespoons of flour and the sour cream to the sauce, mix and then process in the blender.

Return the blended sauce to the pot and add the chicken. Mix well and put dumplings on top. Cover pot and refrigerate it.

Preparation Time: 1 min.   *Cooking Time:* 15 min.

Heat the chicken over a low flame for 15 minutes, turning it from time to time. Do not let the sauce come to a boil. (Heating over an asbestos pad or flame shield will save your having to watch the pot too closely.)   *Serves 4*

Can be frozen

Lickin' Chicken

4 boned chicken breasts   **⅛ teaspoon thyme**
½ cup olive oil   **⅛ teaspoon tarragon**
½ cup Worcestershire sauce   **¼ teaspoon salt**
¼ teaspoon curry powder

The Night Before

Preparation Time: 5 min.

Combine olive oil, Worcestershire, and seasonings. Place chicken breasts in baking dish, turn to coat well, cover, and refrigerate. Turn chicken in marinade once before going to bed, and once again in the morning.

Before Serving

Preparation Time: 4 to 5 min.   *Cooking Time:* 1 hr., 5 min.

Preheat oven to 350°. Place covered baking dish in oven. Bake for 1 hr., basting with marinade once or twice. Remove from oven, run under broiler for 2 min. on each side, and serve.   *Serves 4*

Chicken and Rice Elayne

This dish is susceptible to variation. If you're pressed for time, you can use canned chicken and chicken broth. If you want to make it in tremendous quantities (and it's an ideal buffet dish for a crowd) and economy is important, leave out the chicken altogether and double the frankfurters.

FOR PREPARING THE CHICKEN

1 3-lb. chicken, cut in parts
1 tablespoon salt
¼ teaspoon pepper
1 stalk of celery, with leaves

1 onion, quartered
3 sprigs parsley
4 cups water

FOR THE CASSEROLE

½ cup raw rice
1 tablespoon butter
1 clove garlic, crushed
1 medium onion, chopped
1 can (1 lb.) tomatoes
1½ cups canned spaghetti sauce

1 green pepper, diced
1 can (3 oz.) chopped mushrooms
4 frankfurters, cut in chunks
1 teaspoon salt
¾ teaspoon oregano

The Night Before

Preparation Time: 25 to 30 min.   *Cooking Time:* 1¼ hrs.
                                        (exclusive of preparation time)

Cook the chicken in 4 cups water with the salt, pepper, celery, quartered onion, and parsley for about 1 hr. Remove from pot and cut chicken in bite-size pieces. Reserve 1 cup of the broth.

Brown the rice in the butter until golden, stirring constantly. Add the cup of chicken broth, stir, and then add all other ingredients. Simmer for 15 min. over a low flame and turn into an ungreased casserole. Let cool and refrigerate overnight.

Before Serving

Preparation Time: 1 min.   *Cooking Time:* 1 hr.

Heat oven to 350°. Bake casserole, uncovered, for 1 hr.

Serves 6
Can be frozen

Chicken Breasts Crème Rouge

4 chicken breasts
1 large onion, coarsely chopped
¾ cup chicken broth (or 1 chicken bouillon cube dissolved in ¾ cup boiling water)

3 tablespoons olive oil
1 clove garlic, minced
1 green pepper, diced
1 teaspoon salt
2 tablespoons paprika
1 cup canned tomatoes, **drained**

. . . .

4 tablespoons flour
4 tablespoons light cream

½ cup sour cream

The Night Before

Preparation Time: 15 min.   *Cooking Time:* 30 to 40 min.

In a large, heavy skillet or Dutch oven, sauté the chopped onion in the olive oil until golden—4 or 5 min. over a moderately low flame. Meanwhile, mix together the broth, garlic, green pepper, salt, paprika, and tomatoes. Add these to the onions, cover the skillet, and cook gently for 10 min. Add the chicken breasts, cover, and simmer for 30 to 40 min., or until tender. Remove chicken and let cool before covering and refrigerating. Measure off 1½ cups of the sauce left in the pan, let cool, and refrigerate separately.

Before Serving

Preparation Time: 6 min.   *Cooking Time:* 15 min.
(of which the last 5 min. are in-kitchen time)

Place chicken and sauce in skillet, or, ideally, in a stove-to-table type pot, and heat through. This should take about 10 min. Remove the chicken breasts. Mix the flour and cream together to make a smooth paste, add it to the sauce in the pan, and stir over medium heat until sauce is thickened and smooth. Lower flame, add sour cream, and cook just until heated through. Return chicken to the sauce (or pour sauce over chicken in serving dish) and serve.   *Serves 4*

Chicken Curry

2 tomatoes	2 cloves garlic
1 cup yogurt	3 tablespoons vegetable oil
½ cup sour cream	1 frying chicken, cut into small
½ teaspoon salt	pieces
2 onions	2 tablespoons curry powder

. . . .

1 cup white rice	½ cup raisins
½ cup peanuts	½ cup chutney
½ cup grated coconut	

The Night Before

Preparation Time: 18 min.   *Cooking Time:* 20 min.

Plunge tomatoes into boiling water for 30 seconds, then rinse under cold water and peel and dice them. Mix tomatoes, yogurt, sour cream, and salt together in a bowl; set aside. Peel and chop onions. Peel and mince garlic.

Heat oil in large skillet or stove-to-table casserole. Add onions and garlic and cook just until onions are soft. Add chicken and brown lightly on both sides.

Pour yogurt mixture over and around browned chicken. Cover pan and simmer for 20 minutes, stirring occasionally. Cool slightly and refrigerate.

Before Serving

Preparation Time: 6 min.   *Cooking Time:* 20 min.

Bring chicken curry almost to the boiling point, then cover and simmer for 20 minutes.

Meanwhile, prepare rice and arrange peanuts, coconut, raisins, and chutney in serving dishes.

Serve curry over cooked rice; pass garnishes separately.

Serves 4
Can be frozen at end of night before preparation

Chicken Cacciatore

1 chicken (3 to 3½ lbs.), cut in
    serving pieces
⅓ cup salad oil
2 medium onions, sliced
1 can (1 lb.) Italian tomatoes
1 can (8 oz.) tomato sauce

2 cloves garlic, minced
2 teaspoons salt
¼ teaspoon pepper
1 teaspoon celery seed
1 teaspoon oregano

The Night Before

Preparation Time: 30 min.
                                            Cooking Time: 1¼ hrs.
                                            (including preparation time)

Brown the chicken in hot salad oil. While it is browning, slice the onions and mince the garlic. As the chicken browns, remove it from the skillet and place in a large saucepan or a top-of-the-stove casserole. Place the onions in the oil and cook until golden. Remove the onions with a slotted spoon and add them to the chicken. Drain the fat from the skillet. (If reserving fat for use in another dish makes you feel thrifty and virtuous, save it; if, however, discarding cooking fat makes you feel *slender* and virtuous, go right ahead.) Use the same skillet for mixing all the remaining ingredients. Pour the sauce over the chicken. Cover the saucepan or casserole and cook over a low flame for 15 min. Then uncover the pan and cook for another half hour, turning the chicken pieces over occasionally. Cool slightly and refrigerate, covered.

Before Serving

Preparation Time: 2 min.
                                          Cooking Time: 20 min.

Skim off any fat that has risen to the top of the sauce. Cook, uncovered, over a low flame for 20 min., turning chicken pieces once or twice.

                                               Serves 4
                                           Can be frozen

Oven Fried Chicken

Here's a dish that can be completely prepared the night before since it is at its best cold. It can, however, be warmed.

This will give you slightly more than you really need to feed four people but we suggest you make the full recipe because our families seem to enjoy what's left over in the refrigerator.

3½- to 4-lb. fryer, cut in pieces, plus 1 chicken breast, split
milk
2 eggs
1 cup flour
2 tablespoons dry mustard
1 tablespoon paprika
2 teaspoons pepper
2 tablespoons salt
1½ sticks sweet butter or margarine

The Night Before

Preparation Time: 30 min.   *Cooking Time:* 55 min.

Heat oven to 350°. Put the butter or margarine in a wide shallow pan and melt it over a slow flame.

Pour some milk into one plate and beat the two eggs in another. Put the flour and the seasonings in a paper or sturdy plastic bag.

Dip each piece of chicken into the milk, then into the egg, and then drop it into the bag. Shake the bag well to coat the chicken evenly.

With tongs, dip each piece of chicken into the butter to coat both sides and place the chicken, skin side up, in a large roasting pan.

Bake for 20 minutes, turn pieces, and bake for 20 minutes more. Then raise oven to 450°, turn pieces once again, and bake for 10 to 15 minutes more.

Drain on paper towels and refrigerate.

Before Serving

Preparation Time: 1 min.   *Cooking Time:* 15 min.

If you want to serve the chicken warm, place it back in the roasting pan, cover lightly with aluminum foil and heat in a 350° oven for 15 minutes.   *Serves 6*

Chicken Kiev

6 tablespoons butter
2 tablespoons fresh or frozen chopped chives
1 egg, lightly beaten with 2 tablespoons water
½ cup flour
4 slices white bread

½ teaspoon salt
½ teaspoon paprika
¼ teaspoon black pepper
6 chicken cutlets (or 3 chicken breasts, skinned, boned and split in half)

. . . .

1½ cups vegetable oil

The Night Before

Preparation Time: 12 min.

Cream butter and chives together and place in freezer to firm. Place egg and water mixture in one dish and flour in another. Tear white bread into pieces and make fresh bread crumbs by putting a few pieces at a time through the blender. Add seasonings to bread crumbs and place in a separate dish.

Divide chilled butter-chive mixture into 6 equal parts, and place one inch from one end of each chicken cutlet. Starting from the bottom, roll cutlets, tucking in sides to enclose filling. (Fold the bottom up once to cover butter, then fold sides toward center, then continue rolling up from bottom.)

Dip each piece first in flour, then in egg-water mixture, then in bread crumbs. Place on dish, cover, and refrigerate or freeze.

Before Serving

Preparation Time: 1 min.   *Cooking Time:* 8 to 10 min.

Note: Frozen cutlets should be thawed before cooking; a convenient way to do this is to move them from freezer to refrigerator the night before you want to serve them.

Heat oil to 350° in frying pan. The oil should be about ½ inch deep.

Fry cutlets until browned on both sides, turning once.

Serves 4
Can be frozen

Chicken with Walnuts

This excellent Chinese dish illustrates our point about Chinese cooking being tailor-made for the working cook. Start rice or noodles cooking, toss your prepared ingredients around in a wok or skillet, and you have a fine dinner in 15 minutes.

If you can't find oyster sauce in your local stores, you can order a bottle from one of the mail order sources on page 12. The unused portion can be refrigerated and will stay usable for months.

For convenience, we've divided the ingredients into 3 groups. Prepare each group and refrigerate it in a separate bowl.

GROUP 1

3 chicken breasts, boned and skinned
1 egg white, slightly beaten
½ teaspoon salt
¼ teaspoon white pepper
1 teaspoon MSG
2 tablespoons cornstarch

GROUP 2

3-ounce can sliced mushrooms
½ cup diced bamboo shoots
½ cup sliced water chestnuts
1 package frozen small peas, thawed
1 clove garlic, minced
1 slice fresh ginger, minced

GROUP 3

mushroom liquid mixed with ¼ cup cold water
1 teaspoon cornstarch
1 teaspoon MSG
½ cup oyster sauce

. . . .

1 cup peanut oil
2 tablespoons sherry
½ cup broken walnut meats

The Night Before

Preparation Time: 15 min.

Dice the chicken breasts in ½-inch cubes.

Mix all the Group 1 ingredients in a bowl. Cover and refrigerate.

Drain the mushrooms, reserving the liquid. Slice the bamboo shoots and water chestnuts. Mince the garlic and ginger. Mix all the Group 2 ingredients in a bowl. Cover and refrigerate.

Mix the reserved liquid from the can of mushrooms with ¼ cup cold water. Mix with remaining ingredients in Group 3. Cover and refrigerate.

Before Serving

Preparation and Cooking Time: 15 min.

Take all 3 bowls out of the refrigerator and line them up near your wok or skillet.

Heat the oil to about 300° since you don't want the chicken to cook too quickly. Add Group 1 and mix until the chicken is white. Remove the chicken with a slotted spoon to another dish. Remove all the oil from the pan except about 2 tablespoons.

Turn the heat up slightly and add Group 2 to the pan. Cook for about 2 minutes, stirring.

Add the sherry to the pan, cover and cook for 3 minutes.

Replace the chicken in the pan. Stir, then add Group 3 slowly, stirring. When the sauce has thickened slightly, add the nuts and serve.   *Serves 4*

Coq au Vin

This great chicken-in-wine dish should only be made by a night-before cook. The night that the sautéed ingredients spend basking in the wine in the refrigerator does good things to the flavor—and has the added advantage of leaving you practically nothing to do at dinner time. Since the vegetables are already in the casserole, all you need to go with this is a salad and a becoming air of modesty.

7 slices bacon, diced
4 lbs. chicken breasts, prefer- ably boned
12 fresh mushrooms
12 small white onions
2 scallions, diced
1 clove garlic, minced
12 small new potatoes, unpeeled

3 tablespoons flour
1 teaspoon salt
¼ teaspoon pepper
2 cups red wine
1 cup canned, condensed chicken broth, undiluted

The Night Before
Preparation and Cooking Time: 45 min.

Dice the bacon and sauté it in a large skillet, set at 300° if you're using an electric one. When the bacon is crisp, remove it with a slotted spoon and drain on paper towels. Raise the heat to 375°.

Put the chicken in the skillet and brown on both sides. As the pieces brown, remove them to a large casserole.

While the chicken is browning, rinse and stem the mushrooms, peel the onions, and dice the scallions and garlic. Wash and dry the potatoes and put them aside in a plastic bag.

When all the chicken has been browned and removed to the casserole, put the mushrooms and onions in the skillet, turning frequently to brown. Remove them to the casserole as they are finished.

Add the scallions and garlic to the skillet and cook for about 2 minutes. Lower the heat to about 300° and add the flour, salt, and pepper. Cook, stirring, for 2 to 3 minutes until flour is browned.

Mix the wine and chicken broth together and add to the skillet. Cook, stirring, until sauce comes to a boil. Remove from heat.

Add the bacon to the ingredients already in the casserole and pour the sauce from the skillet over the mixture. Cover and refrigerate the casserole.

Before Serving

Preparation Time: 3 min.   *Cooking Time:* 2 hrs.

Heat oven to 400°.

Add the washed potatoes to the casserole; cover and bake for 2 hours.

Note: This dish can be frozen instead of being refrigerated, in which case it should be thawed before you add the potatoes and bake. We have a tendency to cook more than we need because the leftovers freeze beautifully. The only problem involved in freezing the leftovers is to make sure you have some, and this sometimes involves removing what you hope to freeze before serving the casserole. People who like this dish *really* like it and we've seen the whole casserole demolished by 4 enthusiastic diners.   *Serves 6 to 8*

Can be frozen before potatoes are added

Chicken Anton

Jane Anton, the multitalented source of this recipe, claims that if you slice the cold leftovers of this dish, it makes a great sandwich filling. So far, we have to take her word for this; we've never managed to have any left on the serving dish. This may be another one of those recipes where, if you want any to survive dinner, you'd better hide some in the back of the refrigerator before you ring the dinner bell.

12 Ritz crackers	4 thin slices ham
1 tablespoon minced onion	12 canned asparagus tips
2 tablespoons butter	4 slices sharp cheese
4 chicken breasts, skinned, boned, and halved	grated Parmesan cheese

. . . .

1 cup dry white wine

The Night Before

Preparation and Cooking Time: 15 min.

Crumble Ritz crackers in the blender or pound between sheets of aluminum foil with a cleaver or rolling pin.

Mince onion.

Melt butter in a small saucepan. Add onion and cook until wilted. Add cracker crumbs and mix well.

Pound the chicken breasts flat. Butter a baking pan and lay four of the pieces of chicken in the pan. Place a slice of ham on top of each piece of chicken and top with 3 asparagus tips and then with a slice of cheese. Tuck any ragged end of the chicken breast in so that you have a nice oval shape. Top each with the other half of the chicken breast, again tucking any loose ends under so that you have a smooth mound.

Pat a thin layer of the cracker crumb mixture on top of each chicken mound. Sprinkle with Parmesan cheese.

Cover and refrigerate baking pan.

Before Serving

Preparation Time: 1 min.   *Cooking Time:* 45 min.

Heat oven to 350°. Pour wine around (but not over) the chicken breasts.

Bake, uncovered, for 45 minutes.   *Serves 4*

Chicken Giblet Fricassee

This is a very good and economical dish. You can buy chicken giblets from the butcher or, even more economically, accumulate them in your freezer when you buy chickens for dishes that don't need the giblets. You can use any combination of giblets you like; this happens to be our favorite. Serve with rice or noodles and a salad.

½ cup minced onion
½ cup diced green pepper
½ cup diced celery
8 chicken wings
4 chicken necks
4 chicken gizzards
2½ tablespoons chicken fat or salad oil

2 tablespoons flour
3 cups water
1 teaspoon salt
½ teaspoon pepper
2 teaspoons paprika
½ lb. ground beef

The Night Before

Preparation Time: 40 min.   *Cooking Time:* 1 hr.

Chop onion, green pepper, and celery.

Cut wing tips off and cut wings in half at the joint. Cut necks and gizzards in half. Wash and dry well between layers of paper towel.

Melt the chicken fat or oil in a large saucepan. Cook the vegetables until they are slightly soft—about 5 minutes. Push the vegetables to one side of the pan and add the giblets. Cook until the wings are golden and the other giblets lightly browned.

Sprinkle flour over the giblets. Add water and seasonings. Cover and cook over a moderate flame for 1 hour. Cool and refrigerate.

Form the ground beef into small balls. Refrigerate in a covered dish.

Before Serving

Preparation Time: 2 min.   *Cooking Time:* 30 min.

Add meatballs to the fricassee.

Cook fricassee, covered, over a moderate flame for 30 minutes.

Serves 4
Can be frozen

Chicken and Wild Rice Casserole

No dish using cream, mushrooms, and wild rice could by any stretch of the imagination be called an economy dish. If, however, you feel the need to rationalize this one, it does have its economical aspects. For one thing, it needs no accompaniment other than salad, rolls, and a light dessert, so that the total cost of a company dinner that will make your reputation as a cook is not too high. In addition, you will end up with a pot of chicken soup which can form the core of an inexpensive meal for later in the week. Chicken Egg Drop Soup or Chicken Soup with Matzo Balls (pages 227 and 229) are two good ways of using your leftover soup.

If you need any further rationalization, we point out that this is the recipe we have wearily typed over and over again for guests who wanted it and, on one occasion, dictated the whole thing over the phone to a harried mother who decided it was just the thing she wanted to make in large quantities for her daughter's engagement party.

FOR PREPARING THE CHICKEN

1 chicken, about 4 lbs., cut in parts	1 carrot, peeled
	1 stalk celery
1 large onion, quartered	3 tablespoons salt

FOR THE CASSEROLE

1 cup raw wild rice	1 small can pimento
¼ lb. butter	½ cup chopped onion
¼ cup flour	2 tablespoons chopped parsley
1 can (6 oz.) sliced mushrooms	2 teaspoons salt
1½ cups light cream	

. . . .

¼ cup slivered, blanched almonds

The Night Before

Preparation Time: 25 min. *Cooking Time:* 1¼ hrs.

Place chicken in a large pot, generously covering it with

water. Add the quartered onion, carrot, celery, and the 3 table-spoons salt. Cook for 1 hr. While the chicken is cooking, cook the wild rice according to package directions. You can also chop the onion and pimento and drain the mushrooms, reserving the liquid.

When the chicken is done, remove it from the pot, reserving the broth. Let it cool slightly and remove the meat from the bones, cutting it in ½-inch pieces. Cook the onion in the butter until tender but not brown. Remove from stove; stir in flour. Add enough chicken broth to the mushroom liquid to make 1½ cups. Add this liquid gradually to the flour-butter-onion mixture while heating over a medium flame. Add the cream and cook, stirring, until thick. Remove from flame and add rice, chicken, parsley, pimento, mushrooms, and salt. Turn into casserole and store in refrigerator.

Before Serving

Preparation Time: 2 min.   *Cooking Time:* 30 min.

Heat oven to 350°. Remove casserole from refrigerator, stir contents with a spoon, and sprinkle almonds on top. Place in oven, uncovered, for 30 min.   *Serves 6*

Tongue with Piquant Sauce

1 smoked beef tongue (3 lbs.)   ⅓ cup brown sugar
1 onion, quartered   ¼ cup wine vinegar
¼ cup gingersnap crumbs   1 cup beef bouillon
⅓ cup white raisins

The Night Before

Preparation Time: 12 min.   *Cooking Time:* 3 hrs.
(if your beef tongue weighs either less or
more than 3 lbs., allow 1 hr. per lb. for cooking time)

Place tongue in a large kettle and cover with water. Add the quartered onion and bring the water to a boil. Simmer until done—1 hr. per pound of tongue.

Prepare the sauce by reducing gingersnap crackers to crumbs in the blender or crushing the crackers with a rolling pin; then place the crumbs in a saucepan with the raisins, sugar, vinegar, and bouillon. Stir and let simmer for 10 min. Cool and refrigerate, covered.

When tongue is done, remove it from the pot and let it cool. The skin can then be removed easily by cutting through the underside and peeling the skin off. Remove any small bones from the back and any excess fat. Wrap in waxed paper or foil and refrigerate.

Before Serving

Preparation Time: 4 min.   *Cooking Time:* 5 to 6 min.

Reheat sauce. Meanwhile, slice tongue into quarter inch slices. Serve the tongue slices cold and pass the hot sauce to be spooned over it.

Serves 8 (If you're serving fewer people, you will have enough tongue left over for luncheon sandwiches.)

Danny's Spaghetti Sauce

This is known as "Danny's Sauce" despite the fact that it was a staple of the newlywed Zavins' Friday night open house years before young Danny was born. It acquired its name this way: one night everyone, including the puzzled cook, agreed that the spaghetti sauce was bland and not as good as usual. Investigation proved that Danny had, for many months, habitually tasted and added seasoning to the sauce every time he passed the kitchen while the sauce was cooking. (This also explained why the same recipe seemed to produce considerably *less* sauce than we had been accustomed to having.) On this particular occasion, the sauce had been cooked after our man-for-all-seasonings had gone to bed. At any rate, we like Danny's additions. You can adjust the seasoning according to your taste or that of your own tasters.

1 lb. chopped chuck	1 can tomato paste
1 medium onion, chopped	2 teaspoons oregano
1 clove garlic, chopped	1 teaspoon sugar
1 tablespoon olive oil	½ teaspoon garlic salt
1 can (1 lb.) Italian plum to-matoes	1 to 2 teaspoons salt
	Dash pepper

. . . .

1 package (1 lb.) spaghetti

The Night Before
Preparation Time: 7 min.   *Cooking Time:* 30 min.

Chop onion and garlic and cook slowly in oil until yellow but not crisp. Add beef and cook, stirring, until browned. Add tomatoes, tomato paste, and seasonings. Cook, uncovered, over low flame for 20 min., stirring once or twice.

Before Serving
Preparation Time: 5 min.   *Cooking Time:* 15 min.

Cook spaghetti according to package directions. Skim fat from sauce and heat slowly for 15 min., stirring occasionally.

Serves 5
Can be frozen

Manicotti with Marinara Sauce

If you're foresighted and have made enough marinara sauce (page 77) for your freezer, your preparation time will be cut substantially.

1 box (8-oz.—16 pieces) mani-
    cotti
2 lbs. ricotta cheese
½ lb. mozzarella cheese
½ cup grated Parmesan cheese
2 eggs

2 tablespoons chopped parsley
½ teaspoon nutmeg
4 cups marinara sauce (page 77) or any other tomato or meat and tomato sauce, as preferred

. . . .

¼ cup grated Parmesan cheese

The Night Before

Preparation Time: 10 min. for sauce (page 77)
                30 min. for manicotti
                     Cooking Time: 30 min. for sauce
                             6 min. for manicotti

Boil 6 quarts of water.

While waiting for the water to boil, cut the mozzarella cheese into small cubes and mix together with the ricotta, Parmesan, and eggs. Chop the parsley; add parsley and nutmeg to the mixture.

When the water has come to a rapid boil, add the manicotti—add only a few at a time so the water doesn't stop boiling—and cook for *exactly* 6 minutes. The timing here is important: if the manicotti are overcooked they will be too soft and slippery to fill. Drain into a colander, put manicotti back in pot, and fill the pot with cold water.

Remove the manicotti one at a time and fill each one with the cheese mixture. The fastest method is to use your fingers, but it's also the messiest. If you dislike that cold, squishy feeling, use a knife or an iced tea spoon.

Spread a thin layer of marinara (or other) sauce on the

bottom of a 9″ x 13″ baking pan. Place the filled manicotti next to each other in a single layer.

Pour the remaining marinara sauce over the manicotti.

Cover tightly with foil and refrigerate or freeze.

Before Serving

Preparation Time: 1 min.   *Cooking Time:* 45 min.

Heat oven to 375°.

With foil cover still in place, bake for 25 minutes. Remove foil, sprinkle with Parmesan, and bake for 20 minutes more.

Serves 4 to 5
Can be frozen before baking

Baked Bean Casserole

2 cans (1 lb. each) baked beans
½ cup ketchup
¼ cup molasses
¼ cup brown sugar
¼ cup minced onion
¼ cup green pepper, finely chopped
¾ lb. sliced Canadian bacon (or 5 frankfurters, sliced)
1 orange, sliced

The Night Before

Preparation Time: 8 min.

Place the beans in a shallow casserole. Add all other ingredients except the meat and the orange. Mix well. Lay the Canadian bacon around the edges, overlapping the slices. If you are using frankfurters instead, place the slices in rows around the edges. Place the orange slices in an overlapping row down the center of the casserole. Cover tightly with aluminum foil and refrigerate.

Before Serving

Preparation Time: 1 min.   *Cooking Time:* 35 min.

Heat oven to 375°. Bake the casserole, uncovered, for 35 min.   *Serves 5*

Calf's Liver Dijon

In anticipation of your skepticism when you read this recipe, we'll assure you that neither we nor the typesetter has gone berserk. Admittedly, the combination of ingredients is unusual, if not downright unlikely—mustard *and* garlic *and* onions *and* parsley? On liver? Believe it or not, the final result is not only delicious but also subtle. Be brave. Try it.

1½ to 2 lbs. calf's liver, thickly sliced (about ⅜ to ½ inch)	3 tablespoons parsley, finely minced
½ cup flour	1 scallion, finely minced
1 tablespoon salad oil	1 small clove garlic, crushed
3 tablespoons butter	8 to 12 slices very fresh white bread, trimmed of crusts and crumbed in blender
¼ cup Dijon mustard (a prepared French mustard)	

• • • • • • • • • • • •

5 tablespoons butter ⎱ 2 tablespoons salad oil ⎰	skillet method
or	
7 tablespoons melted butter	broiler method

The Night Before
Preparation and Cooking Time: 17 min.

Mix flour, salt, and pepper and spread out on paper towel or flat dish. Heat butter and oil in large skillet over high heat. Coat liver with flour. Sauté briefly until lightly browned—about 1 to 1½ min. on each side. Remove liver from skillet and set aside.

Mix mustard, parsley, scallion, and garlic together; blend well. Little by little, add the fat remaining in the skillet to this mixture—beat in ½ teaspoon fat at a time. This mixture shouldn't get watery—it must remain thick enough to spread over the liver; if using all the fat would make it too thin, stop adding fat.

Prepare bread crumbs by trimming crusts from 8 to 12 slices (depends on thickness) of *very* fresh, soft, white bread. Crumb the bread in the electric blender (one slice at a time). You should have 3 or 3½ cups bread crumbs. Spread bread crumbs out on a flat surface.

Spread mustard mixture over liver slices, then dip in bread crumbs, coating well. If necessary, press crumbs down lightly with your fingers or with a small spatula. Place liver on a plate with waxed paper in between layers of liver slices. Cover plate with waxed paper or foil.

Before Serving

Preparation Time: 4 min.   *Cooking Time:* 5 to 8 min.

Skillet Method: Melt butter and oil in skillet until fairly hot. Sauté liver slices until covering is nicely browned on each side.

Broiler Method: Preheat broiler. Melt butter in small saucepan. Broil for 2 to 3 min. on each side, pouring half the butter over each side before broiling.   *Serves 4*

Quiche Lorraine

Can be frozen before baking

Rolling out pie crust is an odious chore. Many cooks dislike it, and many accomplished cooks do not do it properly. The Stuart kids learned to curse at an unbelievably early age as they sat in their high chairs watching—and hearing—Mommy bake pies. Mention "Mom and apple pie" to these kids and they'll tell you it's probably some X-rated movie.

There are several solutions to the pie crust problem, some more time-consuming than others. You can, if you're a purist, roll crust out often enough to develop a feel for the whole thing; you'll gain a great sense of achievement and 40 pounds. Or, if you're adept enough at pie crusts but hate to flour the entire kitchen for one little pie, you can prepare ten at a time and freeze them. Another approach (but not for quiche) is to use the somewhat cakey crust on page 247, which is pressed into the pie tin unsullied by a rolling pin. The simplest method, for a cheater, is to use store-bought frozen crusts. Real cheaters can transfer them from their aluminum foil tins to real pie pans, and the truly larcenous can reflute the edges to make the whole thing look slightly messy and homemade.

The timing for this quiche is for the truly larcenous—two frozen crusts are thawed and slightly softened, then pressed into a 9″ pie tin. Cut the two crusts as necessary to fit the pan with a considerably large overlap at the sides, feather the cut edges together with your fingertips, then reflute the shell to form a rather high edge. If you'd rather roll your own, adjust the preparation time accordingly.

1 unbaked pie shell—9″ with deep sides or 10″ with standard sides	1 onion, sliced into thin rings
	½ cup Swiss cheese, cubed
	½ cup Muenster cheese, cubed
8 strips bacon	¼ cup grated Parmesan cheese

. . . .

4 eggs	1 cup heavy cream
1 cup milk	½ teaspoon salt

The Night Before

Preparation and Cooking Time: 20 min.

Preheat oven to 450°. While it is heating, start to fry bacon.

Bake the pie shell for 5 minutes, remove from oven and put aside. Slice the onion and cube the cheese.

When bacon is crisp, remove from pan, drain on paper towels, and sauté the onion in the remaining bacon fat until transparent.

Sprinkle crumbled bacon over bottom of partially baked pie crust. Place the three cheeses on top of the bacon and the sautéed onion on top of the cheese.

Cover with foil and refrigerate.

Before Serving

Preparation Time: 3 min.   *Cooking Time:* 30 to 40 min.

Preheat oven to 450°.

Beat together (lightly—a fork or a wire whisk will do it) the eggs, milk, cream, and salt.

Pour over the bacon-cheese-onion mixture in the pie shell.

Bake, uncovered, for 15 minutes at 450°, then lower oven heat to 350° and continue baking for 15 to 25 minutes longer (it will depend upon the depth of the crust) until set.

Serves 4 to 6
Can be frozen before baking

A Crepe by Any Other Name

This thin pancake rolled around a light filling appears in many cuisines under many titles—crepes, blintzes, palacsinta, and many others. By any name it makes a fine main dish for a summer meal or for a winter one where the edge is taken off the appetite by a hearty first course of soup.

You will note that the recipe will produce about 18 crepes while the filling will take care of only 12. This is not an oversight on our part. It's just as easy to make 18 and if you freeze the extra ones between layers of paper towel and wrapped in aluminum foil, after you've made them a couple of times you'll have enough in your freezer to thaw and use for another meal with little extra trouble.

In any event, if you haven't made crepes before, you may waste a couple from the first batch finding exactly the right ladle or cup that will pour the right amount of batter for your pan and acquiring the knack of pouring the batter with one hand while you tip the pan quickly with your other hand to spread the batter thinly but thoroughly over the entire bottom of the pan.

The preparation time includes the time needed to fill and roll the pancakes after you've prepared the filling of your choice. We've given you two fillings here. You can use many others such as a light seafood or creamed chicken filling.

THE PANCAKES

4 eggs	½ teaspoon salt
3 tablespoons melted butter	¾ cup sifted flour
1 cup water	

. . . .

butter	sour cream

The Night Before

Preparation and Cooking Time: 38 min.

Put all ingredients except flour in medium bowl of electric mixer and mix well. Add flour and mix again until batter is smooth and lump-free.

Heat a small skillet and brush the bottom of the pan with a little melted butter. Pour just enough batter into the pan to cover the bottom, swirling the pan as you pour the batter in. Cook just until the bottom of the pancake is slightly brown and remove the pancake to paper toweling, putting the browned side up. Repeat until all batter has been used. (If you use a Teflon pan, you will not have to continue brushing the pan with butter between pancakes.)

When the filling is ready, place about 2 tablespoons of filling in the center of each pancake, turn the sides of the pancake to the middle and then roll the pancake up from the bottom so that you end up with what looks like a little envelope.

Place filled pancakes on a flat platter, cover with aluminum foil or plastic wrap and refrigerate.

CHEESE FILLING (FOR 12 PANCAKES)

1 lb. pot cheese or drained cottage cheese	¾ teaspoon cinnamon
	1 tablespoon sugar
1 beaten egg	1 teaspoon vanilla
1 tablespoon melted butter	

Preparation Time: 5 min.

Mix cheese and egg together.

Add all remaining ingredients and mix well.

APPLE FILLING (FOR 12 PANCAKES)

4 apples   ¼ cup brown sugar
¼ cup bread crumbs (unsea-   1 teaspoon cinnamon
   soned)   2 tablespoons butter

Preparation Time: 15 min.   *Cooking Time:* 15 min.

Peel apples, then slice and cut into small cubes.

Mix apple cubes with all other ingredients except butter.

Melt butter in saucepan, add apple mixture and cook over a moderate flame for 15 minutes, stirring occasionally. Allow it to cool before filling pancakes.

Before Serving

Preparation Time: 5 min.   *Cooking Time:* 10 to 12 min.

Melt butter in a large skillet (350° if using an electric skillet or griddle).

Place pancakes with the folded sides down in the skillet. Cook for 5 to 6 minutes until underside is nicely browned, then cook the other side.

Serve with sour cream on the side.   *Serves 4*
Can be frozen

Paella

Paella is the perfect party dish for the hostess who is either indecisive or unsure of her guests' preferences. It's a sure bet that a dish containing sausages, chicken, shrimp, clams, and ham has something for everyone. But just to prove that this is an imperfect world, the fates once sent us a dinner guest so deathly allergic to shellfish that she was afraid to touch any part of the paella—the slightest trace of clam liquor on her chicken, she assured us, would send her into shock. She ate a lot of dessert, but everyone else at the party feasted on the parts of the paella they liked best.

Again, the preparation time doesn't include shelling and deveining shrimp. See page 96.

1 lb. shrimp	2 tablespoons olive oil
2 onions	2 dozen littleneck clams
3 gloves garlic	½ cup cornmeal
1 large green pepper	¼ cup olive oil
2 Italian sweet sausages	1½ frying chickens, cut into
¼ lb. boiled ham (unsliced)	small pieces

2 cups white rice	2 cups chicken broth
½ teaspoon saffron	1 cup water
2 teaspoons salt	1 package (10-oz.) frozen peas
1 teaspoon pepper	

The Night Before

Preparation Time: 25 min.   *Cooking Time:* 15 min.

Shell and devein shrimp and refrigerate.

Peel and chop onions. Peel and mince garlic. Seed and dice green pepper. Slice sausages and cut ham into small cubes.

Heat olive oil in skillet and sauté onion, garlic, and green pepper until onion is soft and translucent. Add ham and sausages and cook over low heat for 15 minutes, stirring occasionally. Cover and refrigerate.

Scrub clams with a stiff brush and soak them for 30 minutes in cold water to which you have added the cornmeal. Remove from water, rinse, place in plastic bag, and refrigerate.

Heat olive oil in paella pan and brown chicken pieces on both sides. Cover and refrigerate entire pan.

Before Serving

Preparation Time: 10 min.   *Cooking Time:* 35 min.

Reheat onions, peppers, ham, and sausage in skillet.

Remove chicken from paella pan and set it aside. Reheat the remaining oil in the paella pan and add rice, stirring until rice is golden.

Add onion, peppers, ham, and sausage. Mix well. Remove from heat.

Place chicken broth and water in a saucepan. Add saffron, salt and pepper, and bring to a boil.

Return paella pan containing mixture to heat. Add boiling chicken broth mixture. Stir well. Add browned chicken pieces. Cover and cook over low heat for 25 minutes. Check after 15 minutes and if the rice has absorbed all of the liquid, add another half cup or so of water.

When the paella has cooked for 25 minutes, add the shrimp and frozen peas and stir. Arrange the clams over the top of the paella. Cover and cook for about 10 minutes longer, or until the clams open.   *Serves 12*

Linguini with Clam Sauce

This is a useful party dish. If it's going to be cooked in the same oven with other foods you can bake it at 350° for 30 minutes but please do not bake it at any higher temperature.

1 lb. linguini	1 teaspoon oregano
1 can white clam sauce	1½ teaspoons salt
1 can minced clams	1 minced clove garlic
½ cup salad oil	1 pint (2 cups) sour cream

The Night Before
Preparation and Cooking Time: 15 min.

Cook linguini according to package directions, but decrease the cooking time by 2 minutes. Drain.

Heat everything else except the sour cream together in a large casserole for 10 minutes.

Add drained linguini to sauce in casserole and mix. Add sour cream and mix. Cover and refrigerate.

Before Serving
Preparation Time: 1 min.   *Cooking Time:* 1 hr.

Heat oven to 275°.

Bake, covered, for 1 hour.   *Serves 4 to 6*

Cannelloni with Cheese Sauce

16 lasagna noodles
3 tablespoons butter
3 tablespoons flour
1½ cups chicken broth

¾ cup heavy cream or evaporated milk
salt and pepper to taste
1 cup grated Parmesan cheese

FOR THE CHICKEN STUFFING

1¾ cups cooked chicken, diced
2 tablespoons butter
2 tablespoons olive oil
1 clove garlic, minced
½ small onion, finely chopped

1 egg
2 tablespoons heavy cream or evaporated milk
¼ teaspoon thyme
½ teaspoon salt

FOR THE MEAT STUFFING

3 cups Basic Meat Sauce   (page 18)

The Night Before

Preparation and Cooking Time: 15 min. if using meat sauce
45 min. if using chicken stuffing

Cook lasagna in 6 quarts of boiling water for 5 to 7 minutes. Drain and dry between layers of paper towel.

If you're using the meat sauce stuffing, warm it slightly and skip the rest of this step and proceed to next step. If you're using the chicken stuffing, melt the butter and olive oil in a skillet.

Sauté onion and garlic in butter and oil until golden. Remove from heat. Put chicken through food grinder. (If you do not have a grinder, all is not lost—use a fork and the same technique you'd use for tuna fish salad.) Combine chicken with onions, garlic, and the fat in which they were sautéed. Add egg, cream, and seasonings.

Cut each lasagna noodle into 2 or 3 pieces—each piece should be 3 to 4 inches long. Place a tablespoonful of the filling on each piece and roll into tubular shape. Arrange next to one another, one layer deep, in a buttered baking dish. Set aside.

Melt butter and thicken with flour. Add broth gradually, stirring constantly. Then add cream, salt, and pepper. Cook, stirring, until thickened and smooth. Stir in ¾ cup grated Parmesan cheese. Remove sauce from heat and spoon over cannelloni in baking dish. Sprinkle with remaining cheese. Cover and refrigerate.

Before Serving

Preparation Time: 1 min.   *Cooking Time:* 10 min.

Preheat broiler.

Place 4 to 5 inches from heat and broil for 10 minutes, or until sauce bubbles and top browns.

Serves 6

Cheese Soufflé

Most soufflé recipes cannot be prepared even an hour in advance of baking, much less the night before.

4 tablespoons butter	½ teaspoon dry mustard
4 tablespoons flour	1½ cups grated Cheddar cheese
1 cup milk	4 large eggs, separated
½ teaspoon salt	butter for greasing soufflé dish
¼ teaspoon pepper	

The Night Before
Preparation and Cooking Time: 18 min.

Melt butter in small saucepan. Add flour; cook and stir until well blended. Add milk and cook, stirring, until mixture is very thick. Stir in salt, pepper, mustard, and grated Cheddar. Remove from heat and let cool slightly.

Beat egg yolks until lemon colored and gradually add to cheese mixture. Beat egg whites until stiff. Gently fold cheese mixture into bowl of beaten egg whites.

Turn mixture into greased 1½-quart soufflé dish. Cover and freeze immediately.

Before Serving

Preparation Time: 1 min.   *Cooking Time:* 1½ hrs.

Preheat oven to 300°.

Take soufflé from freezer, uncover, and bake for 1½ hours. Serve immediately.

Serves 6

MUST be frozen

Cornish Pasties

These hearty English meat pies are usually made with pastry dough, and you can do them that way if you prefer. We like the light flakiness of rolled-out frozen patty shells—and the novice who isn't too much of a hand at pastry will find this an easier method.

This recipe makes 6 pasties. One per person is usually enough for a serving. If this is true in your household, freeze the remaining 2 before baking and brush with the egg yolk mixture when you are ready to cook them, increasing the cooking time to 20 minutes at 400° and 50 minutes at 350°.

Move the package of patty shells from your freezer to the refrigerator several hours before you plan to use them. They will roll best if they are not frozen but still cold to the touch.

1 lb. round steak
1 teaspoon Worcestershire
   sauce
1 small potato
1 small onion
1 small carrot
¼ cup minced parsley

2 teaspoons salt
¼ teaspoon pepper
1 package frozen patty shells
   (see note above)
flour
2 tablespoons butter

. . . .

1 egg yolk mixed with 2 tablespoons water

The Night Before

Preparation Time: 40 min.

Cut steak into ½-inch cubes. Put in a bowl and sprinkle the Worcestershire sauce over the meat.

Peel and dice the potato, onion, and carrot and mince the parsley. Add the vegetables and the salt and pepper to the bowl of meat and mix.

Sprinkle a little flour on a wooden board and roll each patty shell out to about a 7-inch circle. Place some of the meat mixture on one half of the circle, keeping it an inch away from the edge. Put bits of butter over the meat and fold the pastry over to close. Pinch the edges together with your fingers and then seal by pressing the tines of a fork around the edges.

As each pasty is finished, use a large spatula to move it to a cookie sheet. Cover with aluminum foil and refrigerate.

Before Serving

Preparation Time: 5 min.   *Cooking Time:* 50 min.

Heat oven to 400°.

Beat the egg yolk and water together and brush the mixture over the pasty surfaces.

Bake, uncovered, at 400° for 15 minutes, then reduce oven temperature to 350° and bake 35 minutes longer.   *Serves 4 to 6*
Can be frozen

Double Duty Recipe: Sweet and Sour Cabbage Soup—Unstuffed Stuffed Cabbage

Stuffed cabbage seemed a "natural" for this book, because it's one of those dishes that demands night-before cooking for the sake of flavor. We had two problems, though: (1) We'd seen people devote a whole evening to preparing it, and since we were not about to spend, or suggest that *you* spend, 4 or 5 hours on one meal, we had to find a simpler way. Shirley Greenwald solved that one for us with her clever notion of leaving the cabbage *un*stuffed—everything is there, the cabbage and the meat are simmered in the sweet and sour sauce, there's no difference in taste, and the whole thing takes 10 minutes to prepare. (2) We needed a good recipe for sweet and sour sauce—the kind Mother used to make. Being the resourceful souls that we are, we took the problem to Dorothy Freeman, who happens to be Mother to half of us, and she gave us her marvelous recipe for sweet and sour cabbage soup.

As given, the recipe is for unstuffed stuffed cabbage. If you wish to prepare cabbage soup instead, omit the starred ingredients and decrease the tomato sauce to ¾ cup.

2 lb. head green cabbage
*1 lb. chopped chuck
*1 egg
*¼ lb. raw rice
*¼ teaspoon salt
1 can (1 lb.) stewed tomatoes
1 cup tomato sauce (see note above)

½ cup vinegar
¾ cup light brown sugar
2 tablespoons lemon juice
1½ cups water
1 apple, cored, pared, and cut into chunks
1 small package (1½ oz.) seedless raisins

The Night Before

Preparation Time: 7 to 10 min.   *Cooking Time:* 2½ hrs.

Cut head of cabbage into quarters, then cut quarters into chunks, shreds, strips, or whatever. Place cabbage into a 6-quart pot. Then add tomatoes, tomato sauce, vinegar, brown sugar, lemon juice, water and apple. If you're making soup, your preparations are over now. Just cover the pot and simmer for 2½ hrs., adding the raisins 45 min. before it's done. If you're cooking this as a main dish, cover and cook over medium-high heat while you prepare the meat mixture. (This will give the cabbage a chance to get slightly soft, so that you can push it down and make room for the meat to float on top of the sauce.)

Mix chopped chuck with egg, raw rice, and salt. Form into meatballs; put meatballs on top of sauce. Cover pot, lower heat, and simmer very gently for 2½ hrs., stirring occasionally. About 45 min. before the end of the cooking time, add raisins.

Before Serving

Preparation Time: ½ min.   *Cooking Time:* 15 to 20 min.

Place covered pot on top of stove and cook over low heat for 15 or 20 min.

If made with meat, this is excellent to serve over rice.

Serves 4

Spaghetti with Oyster Sauce

¼ cup salad oil
¼ cup flour
1 large onion, chopped
1 can (1 lb.) tomato sauce

3 stalks celery, chopped
1 green pepper, chopped
2 cloves garlic, chopped
1½ cups hot water

. . . .

1 lb. frozen, canned, or fresh,
   shucked oysters

½ teaspoon salt
1 lb. spaghetti

The Night Before

Preparation Time: 15 min.   *Cooking Time:* 2 hrs.

Chop the onion, celery, green pepper, and garlic before you begin cooking.

Heat the salad oil in a fairly large saucepan. Add flour gradually, stirring constantly. Add the onion, tomato sauce, green pepper, celery, and garlic. Mix well. Add the 1½ cups hot water gradually, stirring after each addition. Simmer for 2 hrs. This is a fairly thick sauce and is best cooked over an asbestos mat or other flame shield. You can, if you like, start the cooking in the top part of your double boiler and put it over hot water in the bottom part for the 2-hour simmering period. If you do cook it directly over the flame, keep the flame very low and stir frequently to avoid scorching.

When the sauce has simmered for 2 hrs., cool it slightly, cover, and refrigerate in the pan in which it was cooked.

Before Serving

Preparation Time: 5 min.   *Cooking Time:* 30 min.

Cook spaghetti according to package directions. While water for spaghetti is boiling, heat sauce over very low flame for 10 min. Add drained oysters and salt and continue simmering for 20 min.

Place drained spaghetti in a large serving bowl. Pour oyster sauce over the spaghetti and mix well.   *Serves 5 to 6*

Fondue Bourguignon

A fondue dinner requires the participation of your family or guests, who will probably love it. You assemble the components, and everyone spears the meat on a fondue fork, cooks it in bubbling oil, and dips it in one of several sauces. It's a lovely dinner to have when you'd like to spend an hour or two talking at the table—each person cooks, and eats, only one or two bites of meat at a time.

Two practical notes: no more than 6 people can comfortably share one fondue pot, so if you have more guests, use another pot (naturally, we prefer electric fondue pots); a raw potato will keep the bubbling oil from splattering all over you.

1 lb. boneless sirloin steak or sirloin tips
2 chicken breasts, skinned and boned
4 fully cooked sausages (frankfurters may be substituted)
1 cup mayonnaise
1¼ cups sour cream

1 tablespoon paprika
1 tablespoon tomato paste
2 tablespoons fresh dill
1 to 2 tablespoons horseradish
¼ cup prepared mustard
2 scallions, chopped fine
salt and pepper

. . . .

4 cups (approximately) vegetable oil

1 raw potato

The Night Before

Preparation Time: 25 min.

Cut steak, chicken, and sausages into bite-sized pieces. Place in separate plastic bags and refrigerate.

Prepare sauces:

——Mix ½ cup mayonnaise with 1 tablespoon tomato paste and 1 tablespoon paprika.

——Mix ¼ cup mayonnaise and ¼ cup sour cream with 2 tablespoons snipped dill.

——Mix ½ cup sour cream with 1 to 2 tablespoons horseradish.

——Mix ¼ cup mayonnaise with ¼ cup prepared mustard.

——Mix ½ cup sour cream with 2 finely chopped scallions.

Salt and pepper sauces to taste. Store each sauce in a small serving dish. Cover and refrigerate.

Before Serving

Preparation Time: 5 min.

Arrange steak, sausages, and chicken attractively on a platter. Pare the potato.

Heat oil in a fondue pot (it should be about three-quarters full of oil) and place raw potato in pot.

Each person puts an assortment of meat and some of each sauce on his plate, then spears, cooks, and dunks to his heart's content.

Note: The dill sauce on page 79 makes an excellent fondue sauce. *Serves 6*

Monday's Oxtail Ragout

This is called "Monday's" Ragout because, while the time needed in preparation is not great, the combination of the marinating time and the cooking time is too much for a single evening unless you start earlier than is probably convenient. If you plan this for Monday's dinner, however, the time problem disappears. The meat can be marinated Sunday afternoon when you finish the lunch dishes or while you're putting the final touches on your Sunday evening meal. The cooking can then be left for after dinner.

3 oxtails, cut in 2-inch pieces	¼ cup flour
2 cups Burgundy	1 teaspoon paprika
2 large onions, chopped	1 clove garlic, minced
1 carrot, chopped	1½ cups tomato purée
10 whole peppercorns	6 carrots
4 teaspoons salt	3 cups water
3 tablespoons salad oil	

The Day Before

Preparation Time: 35 min.   *Cooking Time:* 2 hrs.

Place the oxtails in a deep bowl and cover with a marinade made of the chopped onions, chopped carrot, peppercorns, 1 teaspoon salt, and the Burgundy. Cover and refrigerate for 3 to 5 hrs., turning every once in a while.

Pare the 6 carrots and cut them diagonally. Wrap in waxed paper or a plastic bag and refrigerate.

When the oxtails have been marinated for the convenient length of time, remove them from the marinade and dry them on a triple thickness of paper towel. Heat the salad oil in a Dutch oven and brown the oxtails well on all sides. Stir in the flour, then add the marinade, the remaining 3 teaspoons salt, paprika, garlic, tomato purée, and the water. Stir and cover. Simmer for 2 hrs. Cool slightly and refrigerate.

Before Serving

Preparation Time: 2 min. *Cooking Time:* 1 hr.

Remove the fat from the surface of the ragout. Pour the carrots into the ragout. Stir, cover, and simmer for 1 hr.

(This goes well with either noodles or mashed potatoes. If your family, like ours, likes to pour the extra ragout gravy over their noodles or potatoes, don't add any butter when you cook them.) **Serves 4**
Can be frozen

Mrs. Albini's Baked Lasagna

Every time our friends, Emilia and Thayer Taylor, have a baby, Emilia's mother, Marion Albini, comes down from Gloversville for a couple of weeks to help out. At some time before she goes home she cooks what she deprecatingly calls "just an old-fashioned Italian dinner" for a few of the Taylors' lucky friends. As a result, these may be the only babies in the world whose birth announcements make the recipients lick their chops in happy anticipation.

Neither of us can duplicate the total effect of Marion's sumptuous dinner. We have, however, had wonderful luck both with this lasagna and with the roasted peppers (see page 204 for the recipe).

THE SAUCE

¾ lb. pork or beef, cut in large chunks
½ lb. Italian sweet sausage
1 tablespoon shortening
1 small onion, chopped
1 clove garlic, chopped
1 tablespoon basil
1 teaspoon oregano
2 cans tomato paste
2 cups water

THE LASAGNA

½ lb. lasagna noodles
1 lb. ricotta or cottage cheese
1 lb. mozzarella cheese, sliced
¼ lb. grated Parmesan cheese

The Night Before

Preparation Time: 30 min.   *Cooking Time:* 2 hrs., 45 min.

Melt shortening in large heavy pot. Add meat and sausage and cook slowly until well browned. Add onion and garlic and cook until golden. Add basil, oregano, and 2 cups water, or more if 2 cups won't quite cover the meat. Allow to come to a boil and then add tomato paste and stir. Lower flame, cover, and simmer for 2½ hrs. Stir occasionally and add water if needed.

During the last 15 min. in which the sauce cooks, prepare the lasagna according to package directions. Heat oven to 350°.

When the sauce is done, remove the meat from the sauce and place meat in top of a double boiler; cover and refrigerate.

In a deep rectangular baking pan or casserole, place a few spoonfuls of sauce. Over this, place one layer of lasagna. Cover with dabs of ricotta, slices of mozzarella, Parmesan cheese, and one quarter of the sauce. Start again with a layer of lasagna, adding the other ingredients in the same order. Make 3 or 4 layers of this. The last layer should consist only of lasagna, Parmesan cheese, and sauce. Bake, uncovered, for 15 min. Remove from oven, let stand for 15 min., cover and refrigerate.

Before Serving

Preparation Time: 2 min.   *Cooking Time:* 20 min.

Heat the lasagna casserole at 350° for 15 to 20 min. Let it stand 5 to 10 min. before cutting and serving. While the lasagna is baking, heat the meat in the top of the double boiler. Serve it separately. (Someone to whom we once gave this recipe made a mistake and put the meat in the lasagna casserole along with the sauce. It came out fine.)   *Serves 6*

Can be frozen

Second-Best Lasagna

We freely admit that this is not as good as Mrs. Albini's lasagna, but it *is* good and can be prepared in less time. We use Mrs. Albini's recipe when we have a long evening for cooking and this one when time is short.

1 lb. chopped chuck	½ lb. sliced mozzarella cheese
1 can (1 lb.) Italian tomatoes	½ lb. ricotta or cottage cheese
1 can (8 oz.) tomato sauce	Enough lasagna noodles to
2 crushed cloves of garlic	make 3 layers in your pan
2 teaspoons salt	(usually a little over ½ lb.)
½ teaspoon pepper	

·   ·   ·   ·   ·   ·   ·   ·   ·   ·   ·   ·

½ cup grated Parmesan cheese

The Night Before

Preparation Time: 18 min.   *Cooking Time:* 45 min.

Put chopped chuck and salt in a saucepan and brown thoroughly, stirring. Add the garlic and pepper and simmer slowly for 10 min. Add tomatoes and tomato sauce, mix, cover, and simmer for 30 min.

While the sauce is cooking, cook the lasagna according to the directions on the box. Drain, rinse with cold water, and drain again.

When sauce is finished, pour one quarter of it over the bottom of a baking dish (12″x8″x2″ is a good size). Arrange a layer of lasagna over the sauce. Top with a layer of mozzarella pieces alternated with spoonfuls of ricotta. Top with a third of the remaining sauce. Repeat the layers, ending with a layer of meat sauce. Cover and refrigerate.

Before Serving

Preparation Time: 2 min.   *Cooking Time:* 30 min.

Heat oven to 350°. Sprinkle Parmesan cheese over top of lasagna and bake, uncovered, for 30 min. Let the casserole stand for at least 5 min. after you have taken it out of the oven before you cut it.

Note: You may, of course, use the basic meat sauce on p. 18.

Serves 6

Chinese Noodles with Bean Sauce

If there is no local market where you can buy sesame oil and bean sauce, try one of the mail order sources listed on page 12. Both will last for months. Just put what you can't use of the can of bean sauce into a covered jar and refrigerate it.

½ lb. ground pork
1 tablespoon peanut oil
3 tablespoons bean sauce
1 scallion, chopped

1 tablespoon sherry
3 tablespoons chicken broth
1 teaspoon sugar

. . . .

1 lb. vermicelli or Chinese
    noodles (lo mein)

1 teaspoon sesame oil

The Night Before

Preparation and Cooking Time: 8 min.

In a small saucepan, sauté the pork in the oil until it is browned, separating the pieces as it browns.

Add the bean sauce, scallion, and sherry and cook for about 2 minutes until the scallion is slightly soft.

Add the chicken broth and sugar, mix and remove from heat. Cool and refrigerate.

Before Serving

Preparation Time: 2 min.   *Cooking Time:* 10 min.

Set a large pot of salted water to boil for the noodles. When the water is boiling, drop in the noodles and cook according to package directions.

Heat the pan of sauce over a moderate flame, uncovered, for about 10 minutes until most of the liquid has evaporated. Add the sesame oil.

Drain the noodles and serve with the bean sauce well mixed with the noodles.

Serves 6

Cheese Turnovers

This is a fine buffet dish; it requires no knife and the pastry crust relieves your guests of the problem of juggling bread separately.

1 package frozen patty shells
¼ cup onion, finely minced
1 clove garlic, minced
1 cup minced parsley
1 lb. cottage cheese, drained
3 tablespoons lemon juice

1 teaspoon dried dill
2 teaspoons oregano
2 eggs
1 teaspoon salt
½ teaspoon pepper

The Night Before

Preparation Time: 30 min.

Let the patty shells stand in the refrigerator or at room temperature until they are defrosted but still cold to the touch.

Mince onion, garlic, and parsley.

Reserve 1 egg and mix all the other ingredients (except the patty shells, of course) in a bowl. Separate the yolk and white of the reserved egg.

On a lightly floured board, roll out each patty shell to about a 7-inch circle. Place about ¼ cup of the cheese mixture on one half of the circle, leaving the outer half-inch uncovered. Brush egg white over the outside of the circle, fold the pastry in half, and seal with the tines of a fork.

As the turnovers are finished, place them on a cookie sheet, cover with aluminum foil, and refrigerate.

Mix the unused egg white with the yolk and refrigerate, covered.

Before Serving

Preparation Time: 3 min.   *Cooking Time:* 25 min.

Heat oven to 450°.

Brush the tops of the turnovers with the reserved egg.

When the oven has reached 450°, place the pan of turnovers in the oven and turn the heat down to 325°. Bake for 25 minutes or until crusts are golden brown.   *Makes 6 turnovers*
Can be frozen

Section Three

ACCOMPANIMENTS

Salads and Salad Substitutes

There are those who will deny that there is any substitute for the mixed green salad. This chapter contains a few convincing arguments against that viewpoint. The Cucumber and Yogurt and the Vegetable Salad, for example, have been known to win high praise from some fairly ardent mixed green salad devotees. But, while you can win some concessions from the salad boys, you will have to include tossed salad in your repertoire and you may as well do it the easiest and best way.

Salad greens may, of course, be washed the night before. The problem is drying the pesky things so that they don't wilt and rust in the refrigerator because of the excess moisture. We have found two good methods. One is the French centrifugal salad dryer which enables you to put your greens in a plastic colander kind of base and with a few twists of the handle whirl them around while the excess water sprays out into the sink. The other method is to reserve a good-sized bath towel for this purpose and put your washed greens at one end, roll the towel over them, put more greens in the next section of towel, and so on until you have one large jelly roll which can be put into the refrigerator. It takes up a bit of room but it works and it's infinitely preferable to patting lettuce leaves dry one by one.

Store your greens in a plastic bag in the refrigerator. Cucumbers, carrots, green peppers, radishes, and such that you plan to include in the salad may be washed, pared, and chopped the night before and refrigerated in a separate plastic bag. You can't slice or quarter tomatoes ahead of time, but that problem has been solved by the fact that cherry tomatoes are now available most of the year. They can be washed the night before and added to the salad at the last minute. Since they do not need to be cut, there is no soggy tomato problem. The greens should be torn into the salad bowl just before serving. The other vegetables and the salad dressing can then be added.

If you have an electric blender, you can with little effort serve a different salad dressing each time even if you serve salad three or four times a week. If your blender is the kind that takes any Mason jar, it is a good idea to buy three or four small Mason jars and make three or four dressings at one time. If the dressing is then stored in the Mason jar, it can be put on the blender for a last-minute reblending just before serving. You can start off with a basic French dressing and then divide it into parts, adding a different flavoring to each part—blue cheese or a few anchovies or some horseradish, parsley, garlic, herbs, onions, scallions, chili powder, or curry powder. If you want a gala twist, add some red caviar to your dressing after blending but before serving it.

Endive Salad

4 endive stalks

· · · · · · · · · · · · ·

French dressing (with horseradish added, if you like)

The Night Before

Preparation Time: 3 min.

Wash and dry the endive, removing any discolored or bruised outer leaves. Refrigerate in a plastic bag.

Preparation Time: 2 min.

Place endive on a wooden chopping board and cut each stalk into 1-inch slices. The endive leaves will separate when you turn the slices into the salad bowl.

Pickled Cucumbers

3 cucumbers, pared and thinly sliced
1 cup sugar

1⅓ cups vinegar
Scant ¼ teaspoon salt
⅛ teaspoon pepper

The Night Before

Preparation Time: 10 min.

Pare and slice cucumbers. Combine sugar, salt and pepper and dissolve in vinegar. Pour the mixture over the cucumbers and refrigerate.

Before Serving

Preparation Time: 1 min.

Drain cucumbers before serving.   *Serves 6*

Green Goddess Dressing

This is not an economy salad dressing but it's very special and well worth a splurge. It makes a fine sauce for fish too.

6 anchovy filets, minced
3 scallions, minced
1 clove garlic, minced
3 tablespoons parsley, minced
2½ cups mayonnaise

4½-oz. can small shrimp
2 teaspoons anchovy paste
2 tablespoons lemon juice
1 teaspoon Worcestershire sauce

The Night Before

Preparation Time: 15 min.

Mince the anchovy filets, scallions, garlic, and parsley.
Put all ingredients in blender and blend for 1 minute.
Refrigerate.   *Makes 2¾ cups dressing*

Mike's Cole Slaw

This recipe is named for Mike Freeman, not because he originated it, but because he loves it so much. And when there's some of it in the refrigerator, it's really *his* cole slaw— no one else gets more than a look at it. Brothers with huge appetites notwithstanding, cole slaw must be prepared at least one day, and preferably two, before it is to be eaten.

Incidentally, people who have eaten only the watery, sourtasting kind of cole slaw commonly served in luncheonettes won't recognize the real thing, which is creamy and delicious.

2 lb. head green cabbage	3 tablespoons vinegar
2 carrots	⅓ cup sugar
1 green pepper	1½ cups Miracle Whip

The Night Before

Preparation Time: 15 min.

Wash and quarter cabbage, then shred it—a knife will shred it well enough, unless you insist on very finely shredded cabbage and want to use a shredder. Shred the carrots with a vegetable parer (or potato peeler). Mince the green pepper. Combine carrots and green pepper with cabbage. Mix vinegar, sugar, and Miracle Whip in an electric blender, or do it by hand, stirring vigorously.

Put half the cabbage mixture into a 2-quart casserole or bowl, then pour half of the dressing over it. Add remaining cabbage and dressing. It may look as though there isn't enough dressing for all that cabbage, but there is; it will drip down through the cabbage and, as it soaks, the cabbage will soften and lose about a third of its volume by yielding its moisture to the dressing. Cover casserole or bowl and refrigerate. Before you go to sleep, and again in the morning if you remember, stir the mixture with a spoon and then press it down with the back of the spoon.

Just check to make sure someone hasn't raided the refrigerator.   *Serves 6*

Vegetable Salad

There are some kitchen chores that are satisfying to the soul and some that are not. In the first category comes stirring things with a wooden spoon. In the second category, for one of us at least, is washing and tearing salad greens. If you share this antipathy, this recipe is heaven-sent. Even if you enjoy the tearin' of the green, you'll find this a pleasant change from ordinary salads.

1 small can sliced beets	¾ cup salad oil
1 small can string beans	¼ cup wine vinegar
1 small can whole carrots	1 teaspoon salt
1 medium onion, sliced	1 teaspoon sugar

(Actually, you can use any combination of vegetables that appeals to you. We try to avoid green peas because their color turns. Practically anything else is fine, though—corn, okra, lima beans—whatever your family likes or you happen to have on hand.)

The Night Before
Preparation Time: 5 min.

Drain the canned vegetables thoroughly. Place in a bowl with the sliced onion and cover with a marinade made of the oil, vinegar, salt, and sugar. Turn vegetables to coat well. Cover and refrigerate. Turn the vegetables again the next morning.

Before Serving
Preparation Time: 1 min.

Drain vegetables and serve.   *Serves 4*

Spanish Salad

This salad is absolutely beautiful to look at and makes a fine addition to the buffet table both because of its appearance and because it does not wilt. You can adjust the ingredients to your taste and the quantity to serve 4 or 40.

enough romaine to form a bed on a large round platter or tray
enough chicory to go around the rim of the platter
green peppers, cut into rings
red or white onions, cut into thin rings

sliced cooked potatoes, fresh or canned
sliced cucumbers
black olives
pimiento-stuffed green olives
olive oil for marinating vegetables

. . . .

tomatoes
olive oil
salt

pepper
wine vinegar

The Night Before
Preparation Time: 18 min. for a very large salad

Wash and dry romaine and chicory. Tear romaine into bite-size pieces, and store in plastic bags in refrigerator. Peel, pare, and slice other vegetables as required. Place each vegetable (olives too) in a separate dish.

Pour some olive oil into each dish and mix to coat vegetables thoroughly. Cover and refrigerate everything.

Before Serving
Preparation Time: 6 min.

About an hour before serving, cut tomatoes into quarters or eighths and marinate in olive oil.

Closer to serving time, place bed of romaine on large, flat platter or tray. Drain vegetables of olive oil, which can be reserved for another use. Arrange vegetables in an attractive pattern on lettuce bed—we like to use a round tray and a kind of wheel spoke arrangement with a section of olives, one of cucumber, one of tomato, etc.

Place chicory around rim of platter. Salt and pepper to taste. (Our taste calls for a lot of salt.) Immediately before serving, splash a small quantity of wine vinegar over the salad.

Caesar Salad

1 large head Romaine lettuce
3 tablespoons olive oil
1 tablespoon lemon juice
1 clove garlic, split
¼ cup grated Parmesan cheese

⅛ teaspoon black **pepper**
¼ teaspoon salt
⅛ teaspoon dry mustard

. . . .

1 egg   1 cup croutons

The Night Before
Preparation Time: 12 min.

Wash and dry lettuce leaves and store whole leaves in plastic bag in refrigerator. Put olive oil, lemon juice, and split clove of garlic into a jar; cover jar, but do *not* refrigerate. Combine cheese, black pepper, dry mustard, and salt in a small dish or other container; cover and refrigerate.

Before Serving
Preparation Time: 4 min.

Note: If no one objects to the sight of raw egg, this is something that can be assembled easily and impressively at the table, as it is done in many restaurants. In that case, all you do in the kitchen is tear the lettuce.

Tear lettuce leaves into salad bowl. Sprinkle cheese mixture over lettuce. Shake jar of olive oil and lemon juice, remove garlic clove, and pour into salad bowl. Break raw egg into bowl and toss salad gently but thoroughly. Bring salad bowl and dish of croutons to the table (even if you are not assembling the whole salad at the table). Immediately before serving, add croutons and toss once more.   *Serves 4*

Snow Pea Salad

If you can't find (or grow) fresh snow peas in your area, turn the page and go on to another recipe. The frozen pea pods can be substituted in some dishes but not in this one, which absolutely demands the crispness of the fresh ones. It's worth going out of your way to get them if you can because this salad is unusual and good.

½ lb. fresh snow peas (pea pods)
½ lb. fresh mushrooms
1 red pepper (nicer color but you can use a green one if necessary)
6 water chestnuts (canned)

1 clove garlic
⅓ cup salad oil
3 tablespoons wine vinegar
1 tablespoon lemon juice
1 tablespoon sugar
1 teaspoon salt

The Night Before

Preparation and Cooking Time: 20 min.

Set a pot of water to boil. Tear the stem tip off the snow peas with a downward motion so you get the string at the side at the same time.

Rinse the snow peas and drop them in boiling water for 2 minutes. Drain, rinse with cold water, and dry between layers of paper towel.

Wash and slice the mushrooms. Stem, seed, and rinse the pepper and cut it in julienne slices. Slice the water chestnuts thin. Mince the garlic.

Combine the garlic, oil, vinegar, lemon juice, sugar, and salt and refrigerate, covered.

Combine the snow peas, pepper, water chestnuts, and mushrooms in a deep bowl. Cover and refrigerate.

Before Serving

Preparation Time: 2 min.

Ideally the salad and the dressing should be combined about 3 hours before serving. If there won't be anyone at home to do that job then, you can do it in the morning. Just mix the dress-

ing, pour it over the salad, and turn the salad to coat the vegetables well.

Drain off excess dressing before serving.   *Serves 6*

Cranberry-Orange Relish

½ lb. cranberries   1 teaspoon grated orange rind
1 cup sugar   ¼ cup water
¼ cup orange juice   ¼ cup slivered almonds

The Night Before
Preparation Time: 10 min.   *Cooking Time:* 10 to 12 min.

Put all ingredients, except almonds, in a saucepan. Cover
and cook for 10 to 12 min. until cranberries burst. Strain juice
off into another pan. Skim the froth off and return juice to
cranberries. Add almonds, cool, and refrigerate.   *Serves 6*

Bean Sprout Salad

1 lb. bean sprouts, fresh or   2 tablespoons sesame oil
    canned   2 tablespoons sugar
½ cup red wine vinegar   2 teapoons salt
2 tablespoons soy sauce   2 teaspoons dry mustard

The Night Before
Preparation Time: 5 min.

Rinse the bean sprouts under cold running water (even if
you're using canned sprouts); drain and pat dry between layers
of paper towel.

Combine remaining ingredients. Place sprouts in a bowl and
pour the dressing over them, turning to coat sprouts.

Cover and refrigerate. Mix again once the next morning.

Before Serving
Preparation Time: 1 min.

Drain liquid before serving.   *Serves 6*

Gelatin Salads

Gelatin salads are what the sportswriters would call "a natural" for night-before preparation. It seems a little futile to give you lots of gelatin salad recipes since the gelatin manufacturers are more than eager to supply consumers with excellent collections of such recipes. Two basic recipes are given here for the primary purpose of indicating the time involved in preparation.

You can vary the vegetables included in your salad. We like combining a small amount of raw, chopped vegetables such as carrots, celery, or green pepper with some canned vegetables. (Try throwing a handful of canned julienne potato sticks in sometimes.) We prefer the gelatin to be a little tart, but you can, of course, vary the seasoning to produce a more bland or even a sharper base.

Incidentally, if the traditional method of unmolding a gelatin salad (dipping the mold in warm water and then running a knife around the edge) doesn't leave you too happy, here's a very safe method you can try. It was suggested by our friend, Marion Brown, whose cooking terminology seems to have taken on a slightly medical air, transmitted, no doubt, from her doctor-husband's office. (Marion is the only woman we know who makes a bouquet garni using medical gauze.) She describes this as "putting hot compresses on the mold." First run a knife around the edge of the mold to separate the gelatin from the sides of the mold. Put a plate over the top of the mold and invert the dishes. Then take a hot towel and press it over the top and sides of the mold. Wet the towel with hot water two or three times. Then place one hand on the bottom of the serving dish and one hand firmly on the top of the mold. Shake once, firmly, and you will find that your salad has unmolded without melting around the edges.

Basic Tomato Aspic

(This can be served either as a plain tomato aspic or with vegetables molded in it.)

1 envelope (1 tablespoon) unflavored gelatin
1¾ cups tomato juice
½ teaspoon celery salt
½ teaspoon sugar
3 tablespoons lemon juice

½ teaspoon Worcestershire
sauce
⅛ teaspoon Tabasco
1½ to 2 cups vegetables (optional)

The Night Before
Preparation Time: 5 to 7 min.

Pour ½ cup tomato juice into a saucepan. Sprinkle gelatin over juice. Heat over low flame, stirring, until gelatin is dissolved. Remove from heat and add remainder of tomato juice and seasonings. If you are making a plain tomato aspic, pour it into the mold, refrigerate, and forget it at this point.

If vegetables are to be added, refrigerate the gelatin mixture until it is slightly thickened. Then add vegetables, stir, and pour into mold. Refrigerate.

Before Serving
Preparation Time: 2 min.

Unmold salad and serve. You can, if you like, serve with salad dressing. Our preference is not to gild the lily. We admit, however, that a little mayonnaise, artistically applied, does dress up the salad.   *Serves 6*

Molded Beet Salad

1 envelope (1 tablespoon) unflavored gelatin
1 can (1 lb.) julienne beets
1½ teaspoons horseradish

½ teaspoon vinegar
¼ cup lemon juice
¼ cup sugar
½ cup celery, finely chopped

The Night Before
Preparation and Cooking Time: 10 min.

Mix gelatin, sugar, and ½ cup water in a saucepan. Heat, stirring, until gelatin is dissolved. Remove from heat. Pour juice from beets into a measuring cup and add enough water to make 1 cup of liquid. Add this liquid and the lemon juice, vinegar, and horseradish to the gelatin mixture. Refrigerate until mixture is slightly thickened; then add beets and celery. Stir well and pour into a mold. Refrigerate.

Before Serving
Preparation Time: 2 min.

Unmold salad and serve.

Serves 6

Cucumber and Yogurt Salad

2 cucumbers, finely diced
1½ teaspoons salt

2 cloves garlic
1 tablespoon fresh or dried mint

. . . .

¾ cup plain yogurt

The Night Before
Preparation Time: 13 min.

Cut the cucumbers into small dice and place in serving bowl.

Place the salt on a wooden board or other firm surface and crush the garlic cloves directly into the salt, grinding them together with the back of a spoon. Sprinkle the garlic-salt mixture over the cucumbers.

If using fresh mint, cut it fine and sprinkle it over the

cucumbers. If you are using dried mint, crush it with the back of a spoon before adding it to the cucumbers.

Toss the cucumbers and seasonings together, blending well. Cover and refrigerate the bowl.

Before Serving

Preparation Time: 1 min.

Add yogurt and toss the yogurt and cucumber mixture thoroughly before serving. *Serves 4*

Baked Spiced Fruit

4 canned peach halves
4 canned pear halves
4 canned pineapple slices
6 maraschino cherries

3 tablespoons butter
6 tablespoons light brown sugar
1 teaspoon curry powder

The Night Before

Preparation Time: 10 min.   *Cooking Time:* 1 hr.

Preheat oven to 325°.

Drain peaches, pears, pineapple, and cherries; then wipe thoroughly dry.

Melt butter in small saucepan. Remove from heat and add sugar and curry powder.

Place fruit in small baking dish, spoon sauce over fruit.

Bake, uncovered, for 1 hour. Cover and refrigerate.

Before Serving

Cooking Time: 30 min.

Preheat oven to 325°.

Take cover off dish and bake for 30 minutes.

Remove from oven, re-cover dish and let stand for 5 minutes before serving. *Serves 4 to 6*

Parsley Mayonnaise

1 egg
1 clove garlic, split
1½ cups parsley
½ teaspoon salt
½ teaspoon sugar
½ teaspoon mustard

⅛ teaspoon paprika
1 tablespoon vinegar
1 tablespoon lemon juice
Dash of Worcestershire sauce
¾ cup salad oil

The Night Before

Preparation Time: 5 min.

Put all ingredients except salad oil into a blender and blend at high speed for about 30 seconds. Switch to low speed, remove blender cover, and gradually add salad oil while the blender is running. When all the oil has been added, continue blending for a few seconds until mixture is smooth. Store in refrigerator in the blender container.

Before Serving

Preparation Time: 1 min.

Blend for a few seconds before transferring the mayonnaise to a serving dish. This is not only a good salad dressing but also makes an excellent sauce for fish.

Marinated Artichoke Hearts

2 cans (14-oz.) artichoke hearts
¼ cup salad oil
¼ cup olive oil
2 tablespoons lemon juice
½ teaspoon salt

¼ teaspoon pepper
1 teaspoon oregano
¼ teaspoon dry mustard
1 clove garlic, split

The Night Before

Preparation Time: 4 min.

Drain artichoke hearts and place in deep, narrow container.

Mix all other ingredients together and pour over artichoke hearts. Stir. Cover and refrigerate. Stir once again later in the evening.

Preparation Time: 2 min.

Pour off marinade and reserve for later use. It is delicious as a dressing for cold string beans and sliced onions.

Arrange artichoke hearts on lettuce leaves to serve as a first course or salad, or cut them into quarters and spear on toothpicks to serve as an hors d'oeuvre.

Serves 4 to 6

Orange, Onion, and Romaine Salad

2 oranges	2 tablespoons lemon juice
2 red onions	2 tablespoons orange juice
1 head romaine lettuce	1 teaspoon salt
3 tablespoons olive oil	½ teaspoon pepper
3 tablespoons salad oil	¼ teaspoon tarragon (optional)

The Night Before

Preparation Time: 6 min.

Peel oranges. Wash and dry romaine. Place oranges and romaine in separate plastic bags and refrigerate.

Peel onions and slice into thin rings.

Combine all other ingredients and pour over onions. Cover and refrigerate.

Before Serving

Preparation Time: 4 min.

An hour or so before serving, slice oranges into thin circles and add them to onions and dressing. Refrigerate.

Just before serving, tear the romaine into a salad bowl. Add the oranges, onions, and dressing and toss.

Serves 6

Dorris Leggett's Cucumber Mousse

½ cup water
1 package lime gelatin
1 large cucumber
1 small onion

½ lb. creamed cottage cheese
1 cup mayonnaise
⅓ cup slivered almonds

The Night Before

Preparation Time: 10 min.

Boil water and dissolve lime gelatin with boiling water. Refrigerate until very slightly thickened.

Peel and grate cucumber and onion into colander. Press juices out with back of wooden spoon.

Fold cucumber and onion and all other ingredients into slightly thickened gelatin. Turn into 4-cup ring mold. Refrigerate.

Before Serving

Preparation Time: 1 min.

Unmold onto serving platter. Garnish with fresh mint, if desired.

Serves 8

Blender Roquefort Dressing

2 cloves garlic, peeled
½ cup crumbled Roquefort or
    blue cheese
2 tablespoons lemon juice
½ teaspoon salt

¼ teaspoon white pepper
1 cup sour cream
6 tablespoons mayonnaise
¼ cup olive oil

The Night Before

Preparation Time: 6 min.

Put garlic, cheese, lemon juice, salt, and pepper in blender and blend at medium speed for 15 seconds.

Add sour cream and mayonnaise and blend at low speed for 15 seconds. Remove top of blender and, with blender running, add the olive oil in a slow stream.

Refrigerate.

Serves 6 to 8

Cucumbers with Sour Cream and Dill

1 cup sour cream   ½ teaspoon salt
1 tablespoon fresh dill, snipped

. . . .

3 cucumbers

The Night Before

Preparation Time: 3 min.

Mix sour cream, dill, and salt together in bowl. Cover and refrigerate.

Before Serving

Preparation Time: 5 min.

About an hour before serving, pare cucumbers and slice thin. Add cucumber slices to sour cream mixture and refrigerate.

Serves 6

Pickled Peppers

Red or green peppers (or a mix-   Oil
    ture of both)   Vinegar

The Night Before

Preparation Time: 5 min.   *Cooking Time:* 20 min.

Cut off and discard the tops of the peppers. Remove seeds and fibers from the peppers. Wash the peppers and place them in a pot with enough water to cover. Cook until tender—about 20 min. Drain and cool.

When peppers are cool, cut them into strips and put them into a jar. Combine oil and vinegar in equal amounts and pour the mixture over the peppers, being sure that there is enough liquid to cover the peppers. Cover the jar and refrigerate.

Before Serving

Preparation Time: ½ min.

Drain peppers and place in a serving dish.

Chick Peas with Dill

This also makes a good hors d'oeuvre.

2 cans chick peas
½ cup sour cream
½ cup mayonnaise
few sprigs fresh dill, snipped
few sprigs fresh parsley, snipped
(1 teaspoon of dried dill

and 2 teaspoons of dried
parsley may be substituted
with satisfactory, although
not equal, results)
½ teaspoon salt
1 clove finely minced garlic

. . . .

lettuce leaves

The Night Before

Preparation Time: 5 min.

Drain chick peas.

Mix remaining ingredients together and add to chick peas. Stir, cover, and refrigerate.

Before Serving

Preparation Time: 1 min.

Arrange on lettuce leaves.

Serves 8

Russian Salad

1½ cups canned mixed vegetables, drained
1 stalk celery
2 scallions (white part only)
2 small sweet gherkins

⅓ cup mayonnaise
½ teaspoon dry mustard
½ teaspoon salt
⅛ teaspoon white pepper

The Night Before

Preparation Time: 8 min.

Drain vegetables.

Dice celery. Mince scallion bulbs and gherkins. Place in a bowl with the drained vegetables.

In a separate bowl, blend the mayonnaise with the mustard, salt, and pepper.

Pour the mayonnaise mixture over the vegetables and mix gently. Cover and refrigerate.

Serves 4

Bean Salad

1 can (1-lb.) red kidney beans	⅓ cup vegetable oil
1 can (1-lb.) chick peas	⅔ cup vinegar
1 can (1-lb.) green beans	¾ cup sugar
1 can (1-lb.) wax beans	1 teaspoon salt
1 onion	¼ teaspoon pepper

The Night Before

Preparation Time: 6 min.

Drain kidney beans, chick peas, green beans, and wax beans and place in a large bowl. Slice onion into very thin rings and add to beans.

Mix all other ingredients together and pour over beans. Stir well, cover, and refrigerate.

Before Serving

Preparation Time: 2 min.

Stir bean salad thoroughly. Remove salad from marinade with a slotted spoon and place in a serving dish. *Serves 12*

Basic French Dressing

1 cup salad oil or olive oil (or a combination of the two)	1 teaspoon salt
	1 teaspoon dry mustard
¼ cup vinegar (wine or herb vinegar if you like)	½ teaspoon sugar
	Dash white pepper

The Night Before

Preparation Time: 5 min.

Put all ingredients in the blender container and blend until smooth—about 30 seconds. If you're making only one kind of dressing, your additional seasonings or herbs can be blended with the dressing. If you want to make more than one kind, add the appropriate seasonings to part of the dressing and reblend for a few sec. Refrigerate in a covered jar.

Before Serving

Preparation Time: ½ min.

Reblend for 10 seconds before serving.

Spinach Salad with Sour Cream Dressing

10-oz. package fresh spinach
2 or 3 cloves garlic
2 tablespoons salad oil
½ pint sour cream

¼ cup tarragon vinegar
½ teaspoon salt
¼ teaspoon pepper

The Night Before

Preparation Time: 5 min.

Wash and dry spinach leaves. Tear into pieces and store in a plastic bag in the refrigerator.

Place split garlic cloves and the salad oil in blender and blend for 20 seconds. Add all remaining ingredients and run blender until they are well mixed. Refrigerate in a covered jar.

Before Serving

Preparation Time: 1 min.

Put spinach in a salad bowl, add dressing and mix well.

Serves 4

Very Russian Dressing

The special twist in this dressing is a large dollop of not-very-expensive red caviar. It needs a few hours in the refrigerator at least to let the dressing absorb the caviar flavor, so don't use it as a last-minute project if you can help it.

1 cup mayonnaise
¼ cup ketchup
1 tablespoon horseradish
1 teaspoon lemon juice
1 teaspoon Worcestershire
    sauce

1½ teaspoons finely minced
    onion
3–4 tablespoons red caviar

The Night Before

Preparation Time: 5 min.

Mince onion.

Put all ingredients except caviar in small bowl of electric mixer and mix until smooth.

Add caviar and mix it in with a spoon.

Cover and refrigerate. *Serves 5 or 6*

Endive and Beet Salad

4 endive stalks   **1 small (8 oz.) can sliced beets**

. . . .

French dressing or oil and vinegar in cruets to be passed at the table.

The Night Before

Preparation Time: 2 min.

Wash and dry the endive, removing any discolored or bruised outer leaves. Refrigerate the endive in a plastic bag. At the same time, put the can of beets in the refrigerator to chill.

Before Serving

Preparation Time: 3 min.

Cut endive into 1-inch slices and place in salad bowl. Add drained beets and toss lightly. The salad dressing may be added before serving, or you can let everyone add his own dressing from cruets of oil and vinegar at the table. *Serves 4*

□ VEGETABLES □

Unless you are a vegetarian, you are not likely to want to spend as much time in the preparation of vegetables as you do on your main dish. For reasons of both health and taste, however, you do want your vegetables to have some variety and appeal. You will find included in this chapter several recipes using those fresh vegetables that take to night-before preparation. Most vegetables are best when cooked briefly just before serving—for those we offer some interesting sauces to be made in advance.

All of these cooked vegetables, except the potatoes, can be frozen, provided you use the Seal-A-Meal freezing bags. (See note on page 8.) Any other method of reheating frozen cooked vegetables tends to result in a dried-out mush. If you use a Seal-A-Meal, however, you may find it worthwhile on occasion to double a recipe and freeze half for the future.

Baked Stuffed Potatoes

You can vary the seasonings when mashing the potatoes according to your whim, diet, or the contents of your refrigerator. Don't, however, omit brushing the potatoes with melted butter before storing. This keeps them moist.

4 baking potatoes, well   2 teaspoons parsley, finely
   scrubbed   chopped
¾ cup sour cream   1 teaspoon salt
1 scallion, finely chopped   2 tablespoons melted butter

    • • • • • • • • • • •

¼ cup sour cream

The Night Before
Preparation Time: 15 min.   Cooking Time: 1 hr.

Bake potatoes in a 400° oven for 50 to 60 min., until soft. Allow to cool.

Cut a slice off the top of each potato. Scoop out the pulp and place in a mixing bowl. Add salt and sour cream and mash potatoes with an electric mixer or a potato masher. Stir in chopped scallion and parsley. Refill the potato shells with the mixture. Brush the potatoes on all sides with melted butter. Place in a baking dish, cover with waxed paper or aluminum foil and refrigerate.

Before Serving

Preparation Time: 1 min.   *Cooking Time:* 20 min.

Heat oven to 350°. Bake potatoes, uncovered, for 20 min. Before serving, put an additional dollop of sour cream on top of each potato or pass the sour cream separately.

Serves 4

Baked Stuffed Mushrooms

1 lb. fresh mushrooms	⅓ cup seasoned bread crumbs
3 tablespoons butter	1½ tablespoons butter (for dot-
1 tablespoon minced parsley	ting)
1 egg, lightly beaten	

The Night Before
Preparation and Cooking Time: 10 min.

Wash and dry mushrooms. Remove stems and chop them. Sauté stems in butter for 4 or 5 min. Remove from heat, add parsley, egg, and bread crumbs. Toss until well mixed. Spoon some of this mixture into the hollow of each mushroom cap. Place mushrooms in a shallow, lightly buttered baking dish. Dot with butter, cover, and refrigerate.

Before Serving
Cooking Time: 20 min.

Place uncovered baking dish in a cold oven. Set heat control at 350° and bake for 20 min.   *Serves 4*

Buttered String Beans

If you are willing to live dangerously and sacrifice a few vitamins for a great deal of taste, try this method of preparing string beans. Contrary to everything you have always read about cooking vegetables in as little water as possible and serving them immediately, this recipe calls for 6 quarts of boiling water, rapid cooling, and refrigeration. As unlikely as it sounds, the string beans are greener, crunchier, and tastier than those cooked by traditional methods.

6 quarts boiling water	2 to 3 tablespoons butter or
1 lb. green (string) beans	margarine

The Night Before

Preparation Time: 12 min.   Cooking Time: 7 min.

Bring 6 quarts of water to a rapid boil. Meanwhile, wash and trim the string beans. We prefer them left whole, but cut them to any size you like. On occasion, we have shortened the preparation time to almost zero by not trimming the ends—they taste just as delicious.

Plunge the string beans into the rapidly boiling water and boil for exactly 7 minutes.

Immediately drain in colander and run cold water over beans to stop the cooking. Keep the cold water running until you are quite sure all of the beans are cool—this process keeps them green and crunchy.

Place butter, cut into several pieces, in bottom of wide, shallow saucepan. Place drained, cooled string beans on top. Cover and refrigerate. (Note: these may be refrigerated for up to 24 hours; if kept longer than that, the texture suffers.)

Before Serving

Preparation Time: 1 min.   Cooking Time: 10 min.

Heat beans in covered pan over medium heat, shaking frequently, for 5 minutes. Remove cover and cook another few minutes until heated through.

Serves 4

Baked Butternut Squash

2 butternut squash   6 tablespoons brown sugar
4 tablespoons butter or marga-
   rine

The Night Before

Preparation Time: 3 min.

Cut squash vertically into symmetrical halves. Scoop out seeds. Arrange in baking dish.

Place 1 tablespoon butter and 1½ tablespoons brown sugar into each cavity. Cover and refrigerate.

Before Serving

Preparation Time: 1 min.   *Cooking Time:* 1 hr.

Heat oven to 375°.

Bake squash, uncovered, until tender—about 1 hour. After 15 minutes of baking, spoon a little of the liquid from the cavities over the entire surface of the squash.   *Serves 4 to 6*

Oregano Potatoes

Canned potatoes are not perfect substitutes for fresh ones—they are somehow denser and less delicate. However, the cook-in-a-hurry can make a can of potatoes taste delicious by sautéeing them until they are crusty.

½ cup butter   1 tablespoon oregano
1 large can tiny whole potatoes

Before Serving

Preparation and Cooking Time: 15 min.

Melt butter in skillet. Drain potatoes.

Sauté potatoes and oregano over low heat until potatoes are well browned.   *Serves 6*

Pickled Vegetables

These pickled vegetables will take you less than half an hour to make and must then be refrigerated for a week before you use them. Among their other virtues, they will last indefinitely in the refrigerator and make a fine emergency hors d'oeuvre and a very attractive garnish. Incidentally, they taste good too!

One word of caution: you may find the hard way that your hands are sensitive to the oils in chili peppers. Seed them under cold running water, preferably wearing plastic gloves. Let them stay in your jar but don't serve them; they're fine for flavoring but too strong for anyone without an asbestos-lined esophagus to eat.

2 cups sugar	2 red or green peppers
2 cups white vinegar	3 carrots
1 cup water	½ lb. white radish
2 teaspoons salt	2 chili peppers (see note above)
1 medium cauliflower	

Preparation and Cooking Time: 25 min.

Combine sugar, vinegar, water, and salt in a saucepan and bring to a boil. Remove from stove and let cool.

Boil a large pot of water for blanching the vegetables.

Cut the cauliflower into individual flowerets. Peel the carrots and radish and cut them into pieces about 1″ by ½″. These are particularly attractive if you use a French-fry cutter.

Stem and seed the peppers and cut them into 1″ squares. Split the chili peppers lengthwise and seed them under running water. (See note above.)

Drop all the vegetables in the boiling water, turn off the heat and let them stand for 2 minutes. Drain and pat them dry with paper towels.

Pack the vegetables in a large container, pour the marinade over them, and refrigerate for a week before using.   *Serves 12*

Individual Noodle Puddings

Rose Lubin, who gave us this recipe, used corkscrew noodles. We prefer fine noodles but we rather suspect it will work well with whatever kind you happen to have on your cupboard shelf when the urge to make the dish hits you.

These can be made completely in advance and either refrigerated or frozen for later use. In either case, bring to room temperature and heat, lightly covered with aluminum foil, in a 350° oven for 10 to 12 minutes.

½ lb. fine noodles
1 cup cottage cheese
3 eggs
½ cup marmalade or pear,
    peach, or apricot preserves

½ teaspoon salt
1 teaspoon vanilla
1½ tablespoons butter

The Night Before

Preparation Time: 10 min.   *Cooking Time:* 10 min.

Cook noodles according to package directions. Drain and rinse with cold water.

While noodles are cooking, put small piece of butter in each cup of a muffin pan and place in warm oven until butter melts.

Beat eggs.

Mix all ingredients in a large bowl. Divide the mixture among the muffin cups.

Cover muffin pan with foil or plastic wrap and refrigerate.

Before Serving

Preparation Time: 1 min.   *Cooking Time:* 1 hr.

Remove muffin tin from refrigerator and bring to room temperature.

Heat oven to 350°.

Bake for 1 hour.   *12 individual puddings*

Sweet Potato—Carrot Bake

Any reader with a good Jewish cook in her background will recognize this for what it is—a "tsimis." It's the carrot dish for people who think they don't like cooked carrots.

3 sweet potatoes (about 1¾ lbs.) 1 tangerine or ½ orange
5 medium or 4 large carrots ½ cup brown sugar
. . . .
4 tablespoons melted butter

The Night Before

Preparation Time: 18 min. *Cooking Time:* 30 min.

Boil a large pot of water for the potatoes and a smaller one for the carrots. Wash the potatoes and drop them in the boiling water for 25 minutes.

Scrape the carrots and cut them in ½-inch slices. Drop them in boiling water for 10 minutes. Drain.

Remove the potatoes from the pot and allow them to cool until they can be peeled comfortably. Cut each potato in quarters lengthwise and then in ½-inch slices.

Wash and dice the tangerine or half orange, including the peel. Discard pits.

Mix the carrots, potatoes, orange, and brown sugar together and transfer to a buttered casserole. Refrigerate, covered.

Before Serving

Preparation Time: 2 min. *Cooking Time:* 1 hr.

Heat oven to 350°. Melt butter in a small pan.

Pour melted butter over vegetable mixture and mix gently.

Bake, uncovered, for 1 hour. *Serves 6*

Potato Casserole

This is a most useful recipe. It is a hearty and satisfying

potato dish that can be made into a really good poultry stuffing by doubling the amount of bread.

4 large potatoes	½ teaspoon pepper
4 slices bread	1 onion
1 egg	¼ cup butter, margarine, or bacon fat
1 teaspoon salt	

The Night Before
Preparation and Cooking Time: 19 min.

Peel and quarter potatoes. Boil until tender.

Lightly toast bread. Cut into small cubes and set aside.

Mash potatoes with egg, salt, and pepper.

Peel and mince onion.

Cook onions in butter or bacon fat in large skillet until soft. Add bread crumbs and cook, tossing, for 2 or 3 minutes.

Combine bread and potatoes. Turn into a lightly greased casserole dish, cover, and refrigerate.

Before Serving
Preparation Time: 1 min.   *Cooking Time:* 30 min.

Heat oven to 350°.

Bake for 15 minutes with cover on and 15 minutes with cover off. Note: cooking time will vary with the shape of the casserole dish—a wide, shallow dish will require less time than a deeper one.   *Serves 6*

Baked Beans

Canned baked beans can have the edge taken off their rather prosaic character by using the recipe for Baked Bean Casserole (page 143). If you are using this as a side dish, rather than as a main course, eliminate the meat and the orange. Cut the rest of the ingredients in half and you will have an adequate serving for 4 people. The night-before preparation time will be reduced to about 6 min. and you can reduce the cooking time before serving to 30 min.

Vegetable Potpourri

We tend to use this as a company dish—first, because it enables you to use fresh vegetables in an unusual and delicious stew that does not need to be prepared just before serving and, second, because we've never been able to figure out what you'd do with the other half of the eggplant if you tried cutting the recipe in half. You can, however, freeze the cooked portion you don't use.

3 cloves garlic, chopped	2 green peppers, cut in 2-inch
1 large onion, sliced	chunks
¼ cup olive oil	4 tomatoes, cut in eighths
2 zucchini, pared and sliced	¼ cup water
1 small eggplant, peeled and	3 tablespoons flour
cubed	

. . . .

2 teaspoons salt	2 tablespoons capers
¼ teaspoon pepper	

The Night Before

Preparation Time: 22 min. *Cooking Time:* 1 hr., 15 min.

Slice the onion and mince garlic.

Heat the olive oil in a large, heavy pan. Sauté the garlic and onion, over low heat, until yellow but not crisp.

While this is cooking, pare and slice the zucchini; peel and cube the eggplant; wash, seed, and cut the green peppers in cubes. Put these vegetables in a bag with the flour and shake well until the pieces are lightly coated with flour.

When the onion is yellow, add the eggplant, zucchini, peppers, and the ¼ cup water.

Stir well, cover, and cook over low flame for 1 hour.

Wash the tomatoes and cut them in eighths. After the vegetables have cooked for an hour, add the tomatoes and stir well. Cook 15 minutes longer, then remove from heat and refrigerate, covered.

Preparation Time: 3 min. *Cooking Time:* 15 min.

Add the salt, pepper, and capers.

Simmer, uncovered, for 15 minutes, stirring occasionally.

Serves 8

Polish Potatoes

3 potatoes (about 1½ lbs.)
3 tablespoons minced onion
2 slices thick bacon, cut in ½-inch pieces
2 tablespoons butter, room temperature

1 egg
¼ cup milk
1 teaspoon salt
¼ teaspoon white pepper

The Night Before

Preparation Time: 12 min. *Cooking Time:* 20 min.

Boil a pot of water for the potatoes. Peel and quarter the potatoes and cook them in boiling water for 20 minutes. Drain.

While the potatoes are cooking, mince the onion and dice the bacon.

Put the potatoes, egg, milk, butter, salt, and pepper in the bowl of the electric mixer and beat until smooth. Add the minced onion and mix again.

Turn the potatoes into a 1-quart casserole and lay bacon pieces over the top. Cover and refrigerate.

Before Serving

Preparation Time: 1 min. *Cooking Time:* 30 min.

Heat oven to 400°.

Bake casserole uncovered, for 30 minutes. (Note: if you're cooking something in the oven at the same time which requires a lower temperature than 400°, you can bake the potato casserole at the lower heat and then if necessary run it under the broiler for a few minutes to crisp the bacon.) *Serves 4*

Red Cabbage

The secret of this red cabbage is that it is cooked in wine—not vintage wine, just any red wine you happen to have around. It's another of those dishes that improve in flavor by being allowed to rest in the refrigerator overnight—or longer.

2 lbs. red cabbage
2 medium apples, peeled and cubed
1 large onion, spiked with 10 to 12 cloves

2 tablespoons butter
2 cups red wine
1 teaspoon salt
¼ teaspoon pepper
1 bay leaf

The Night Before

Preparation Time: 12 min.   *Cooking Time:* 1½ hrs.

Rinse and dry cabbage and cut into the thinnest slices possible.

Peel and cube apples. Peel onion and spike with cloves.

Put all ingredients in a large saucepan and cook gently for 1½ hours, stirring occasionally.

Before Serving

Preparation Time: 1 min.   *Cooking Time:* 5 min.

Reheat over moderate flame.

Remove and discard onion and bay leaf before serving.

Serves 8 to 10

Zucchini Casserole

2 tablespoons butter
4 to 5 small zucchini (about 3 cups when sliced)

2 medium onions, sliced
1 can (1 lb.) stewed tomatoes

· · · · · · · · · · · ·

Grated cheese

The Night Before

Preparation and Cooking Time: 15 min.

Sauté the sliced onions in the melted butter until golden. Meanwhile, pare and slice the zucchini. Remove onions from stove, stir in sliced zucchini and stewed tomatoes. Cover and refrigerate.

Before Serving

Preparation Time: 1 min.   *Cooking Time:* 45 min.

Heat oven to 350°. Sprinkle grated cheese liberally over top of casserole, completely covering the other ingredients. Bake, uncovered, for 45 min.   *Serves 5 to 6*

Corn Fritters

1½ cups corn kernels, canned or freshly scraped from corn on the cob

2 eggs

¾ cup flour
1 teaspoon baking powder
½ teaspoon salt

. . . .

2 tablespoons butter
2 tablespoons vegetable oil

maple syrup

The Night Before

Preparation Time: 4 min.

Place corn and eggs in container of electric blender. Blend on low speed for 2 or 3 seconds. Store container in refrigerator.

Toss flour, baking powder, and salt together in small bowl. Cover.

Before Serving
Preparation and Cooking Time: 6 min.

Melt butter and oil together in large, heavy skillet.

Add flour mixture to corn-egg mixture in blender container and blend just until flour disappears—about half a second.

Pour about ¼ cupful of batter per fritter into hot fat and fry, turning once, until golden brown on both sides. Serve hot with maple syrup.   *Serves 4*

Hashed Brown Potatoes

4 medium potatoes	1¼ teaspoons salt
3 tablespoons grated onion	Dash of pepper

. . . .

3 tablespoons bacon fat or salad oil	3 tablespoons butter

The Night Before

Preparation Time: 13 min.   *Cooking Time:* 30 min.

Peel potatoes and cook in boiling water for 25 to 30 min. Chill and then grate potatoes and onion into a large bowl. Add salt and pepper, tossing very lightly. Cover and refrigerate.

Before Serving

Preparation Time: 5 min.   *Cooking Time:* 20 min.

If you're using an electric skillet, heat it to 300° before putting in the butter and bacon fat or salad oil. If you're using a nonelectric skillet, melt the fats in the skillet over a medium flame. When the fat bubbles, pour the potatoes into the pan and flatten them with a spatula. Shape the potatoes into a circle with the spatula, leaving a ¾-inch trough between the potatoes and the edge of the pan. Cook 20 min., then cut the potatoes from the edge of the pan to the center. Turn the two cut quarters over the uncut half and slide the whole thing onto a platter. *Serves 4*

Mashed Potatoes and Turnips

4 large potatoes	½ cup milk
1 small yellow turnip (rutabaga)	1 teaspoon salt
¼ cup butter	½ teaspoon pepper

The Night Before

Preparation Time: 15 min.   *Cooking Time:* 30 min.

Peel and cube turnips and potatoes. Cook in boiling water

until tender—30 minutes for turnips and 15 for potatoes. Drain.

Mash turnips and potatoes together with butter and milk. (This is most easily done with an electric beater.) Add salt and pepper.

Place mixture in a baking dish. Cover and refrigerate.

Before Serving

Cooking Time: 20 min.

Preheat oven to 350°.

Heat for 15 minutes with cover on. Remove cover and heat for 5 minutes longer—or until heated through—with cover off.

Serves 6

Honeyed Carrots

1 bunch carrots	½ teaspoon salt
6 tablespoons honey	2 teaspoons lemon juice

· · · · · · · · · · · · ·

1 tablespoon flour	1 tablespoon melted butter

The Night Before

Preparation Time: 12 min.   *Cooking Time:* 1 hr.

Scrape the carrots and cut them into ¼-inch slices. Place in a saucepan with water to cover. Bring to a boil, then reduce heat and cook for 10 min. Add honey, lemon juice, and salt to liquid in pan; stir well. Cook slowly, uncovered, until liquid has been reduced by half. This will take about 45 to 50 min. Cool, cover, and refrigerate.

Before Serving

Preparation Time: 3 min.   *Cooking Time:* 6 min.

Start warming the carrots over a low flame. Meanwhile, melt the butter and blend the flour into it. Add the butter-flour mixture to the carrots. Cook, stirring occasionally, until the mixture comes to a boil. Cook for 1 min. more over a low flame.

Serves 4

Caesar Green Beans

1½ tablespoons salad oil or olive oil
1½ tablespoons wine vinegar

2 teaspoons minced onion
¼ teaspoon salt

. . . .

1 can (1 lb.) whole string beans
¾ cup croutons

3 tablespoons grated Parmesan cheese

The Night Before

Preparation Time: 5 min.

Mince onion and mix it with oil, vinegar, and salt. Store, covered, in refrigerator.

Before Serving

Preparation Time: 2 min.   *Cooking Time:* 5 min.

Drain beans and place in saucepan. Pour the oil-vinegar-onion mixture over beans. Add croutons. Stir well and cook until hot. Remove from heat and stir in Parmesan cheese.

Serves 4

Baked Tomatoes

4 tomatoes
salt
pepper
2 tablespoons brown sugar

1 green pepper
3 scallions
butter

The Night Before

Preparation Time: 12 min.

Butter the bottom of a baking dish large enough to hold 8 tomato halves, side by side.

Cut each tomato in half crosswise and place the tomatoes, cut side up, in the baking dish. Sprinkle with salt, pepper, and brown sugar.

Slice scallions thin and dice green pepper. Sprinkle over top of tomatoes. Dot with butter.

Cover the baking pan with aluminum foil and refrigerate.

Before Serving

Preparation Time: 1 min.   *Cooking Time:* 20 min.

Heat oven to 350°.

Bake tomatoes, uncovered, for 20 minutes.   *Serves 4*

Baked Wild Rice

3 tablespoons butter
1 green pepper, finely chopped
1 cup wild rice
1 teaspoon salt

2¾ cups canned chicken broth
(or half water, half chicken
broth)

The Night Before
Preparation and Cooking Time: 10 min.

Chop green pepper. Melt butter in saucepan and cook green pepper in the butter for 3 min., stirring occasionally. Meanwhile, grease the bottom and sides of a 2-quart casserole.

When green pepper has sautéed for 3 min., add the salt, rice, and chicken broth. Mix and turn into the greased casserole. Cover and refrigerate.

Before Serving
Preparation Time: 1 min.   *Cooking Time:* 1 hr.

Heat oven to 325°. Stir contents of casserole once, re-cover and place in oven. Bake for 1 hr.   *Serves 6*

Italian Roasted Peppers

3 large green or red peppers
1 clove garlic
¼ bottle pine nuts
¼ cup pitted black olives, cut in pieces

½ cup flavored bread crumbs
¼ cup olive oil
½ teaspoon salt
⅛ teaspoon pepper

The Night Before

Preparation Time: 10 min.   *Cooking Time:* 35 to 40 min.

Heat oven to 350°. Cut peppers in strips, removing seeds, and place in shallow baking pan. Add chopped garlic, nuts, olives, salt, and pepper and mix. Sprinkle bread crumbs over mixture and pour oil over top. Bake, uncovered, at 350°, for 35 to 40 min., stirring occasionally. Store in refrigerator.

Before Serving

Preparation Time: 1 min.   *Cooking Time:* 5 to 10 min.

The peppers can be reheated either in the oven at 300° for 10 min. or in a saucepan on top of the stove for about 5 min.

Serves 6

Eggplant Casserole

1 medium eggplant
2 cups canned tomatoes
1 green pepper
1 medium onion
3 tablespoons butter

3 tablespoons flour
1½ teaspoons salt
1 tablespoon brown sugar
Bread crumbs
Grated cheese

The Night Before

Preparation and Cooking Time: 25 min.

Peel and dice the eggplant. Cook for 10 min. in boiling water. While it is cooking, chop the tomatoes, onion, and pepper.

Melt the butter and add the flour, stirring. Add the tomatoes, pepper, onion, salt, and sugar. Cook for 5 min.

Drain the eggplant and place it in a greased 1-quart casserole. Top with vegetable mixture. Cover lightly with bread crumbs and sprinkle with grated cheese. Cover and refrigerate.

Before Serving

Preparation Time: 1 min.   *Cooking Time:* 35 min.

Bake, uncovered, in 350° oven for 35 min.   *Serves 5 to 6*

See also: Three-Way Eggplant (page 239).

☐ VEGETABLE SAUCES ☐

Almost all green vegetables are at their best when they are cooked just before serving. As a general approach, we suggest that you do whatever is necessary to prepare vegetables for cooking—washing, drying, trimming, paring—the night before, then refrigerate them in plastic bags. If you want to dress cooked vegetables with something more than butter, salt, and pepper, try these sauces. Only the cheese sauce lends itself to night-before preparation, but the others take so little time and effort that you won't mind doing them just before serving. You can also, of course, use the sauces over canned or frozen vegetables as well as fresh ones.

Swiss, Parmesan, or Cheddar Cheese Sauce

1 tablespoon butter
1 tablespoon flour
½ cup chicken broth

¼ cup heavy cream
¼ cup grated Swiss, Parmesan, or Cheddar cheese

The Night Before
Preparation and Cooking Time: 6 min.

Melt butter, stir in flour, and cook until smooth.

Gradually add chicken broth and cream, stirring constantly until thickened.

Remove from heat and stir in grated cheese. Cover and refrigerate.

Before Serving
Preparation and Cooking Time: 5 min.

Reheat sauce over very low heat, stirring constantly. Serve over freshly cooked green vegetables or in *au gratin* preparations of broccoli or cauliflower.

Butter and Almond Sauce

½ cup butter   1 tablespoon lemon juice
¼ cup sliced almonds

Before Serving
Preparation and Cooking Time: 3 min.

Sauté almonds in butter until golden brown.
Stir in lemon juice.

. . . .

Blender Hollandaise Sauce

¼ cup butter   1½ tablespoons lemon juice
1 egg yolk   ⅛ teaspoon paprika
⅛ teaspoon salt

Before Serving
Preparation and Cooking Time: 6 min.

Melt butter.

Mix egg yolk and salt in blender for just an instant, then add other ingredients. Blend until sauce is thick and perfectly smooth.

Heat in top of double boiler, being careful not to let sauce get so hot that it curdles.

See also Three-Way Eggplant, page 239.

. . . .

Chive-Lemon Butter Sauce

½ cup butter   2 tablespoons fresh or frozen
¼ cup lemon juice   chopped chives

Before Serving

Preparation and Cooking Time: 3 min.

Place all ingredients in small saucepan and cook over low heat until butter is melted and bubbly.

Serve over cooked asparagus, artichokes, broccoli, brussels sprouts.

□ BREAD □

If you live or work in the vicinity of a good bakery, you have the bread problem licked. You may not, however, have the weight problem solved, as one of us who has a superb bakery at each end of the subway between home and office can testify! If you lack the irresistible bakery, this is one area in which the frozen food counter of your market can help. There are some good frozen rolls and breads available and we've indicated in this chapter some ideas on how to use these or fully baked bread and rolls if you want to dress them up a bit.

We've also, however, led you into temptation with a few recipes for homemade bread that can be made the night before and one recipe for popovers that takes less time than mixing your salad. There's something very special about homemade bread—so special that all it takes to make a memorable meal is a good soup, the bread, and dessert.

The oldest of the four children we have between us has long espoused the theory that the ideal gift is one that opens doors for the recipient. If these bread recipes do it for you—Happy Birthday!

SOME SHORTCUTS: USING BROWN-AND-SERVE FRENCH BREAD OR ROLLS

Split, but do not separate, bread or rolls through the middle and spread each half with any one of the following. Then close into original shape, wrap securely with foil or plastic wrap, and refrigerate. Before serving, brown according to package directions.

Garlic and Parmesan Bread

1 stick (¼ lb.) butter   Grated Parmesan cheese
2 cloves garlic, crushed

Cream softened butter with crushed garlic. Spread on bread; sprinkle Parmesan cheese on each half.

Anchovy Bread

1 stick (¼ lb.) butter   1 tablespoon anchovy paste

Cream softened butter with anchovy paste. Spread on bread.

USING FULLY BAKED BREAD OR ROLLS

Cut French bread into rounds, or split rolls through the middle. Spread with any one of the mixtures suggested above; or spread with softened butter, then top each round with one of the following:

Dried oregano
Cinnamon and sugar
Chopped olives
Minced green pepper
Rolled anchovy filet

Place rounds in a baking dish or on a cookie sheet, cover with foil or waxed paper, and refrigerate. Before serving, heat in oven at 350° for about 10 min. (A special, but not absolutely necessary, touch when using cinnamon and sugar is to run it under the broiler for the last minute or two.) Serve hot.

Fried Garlic Bread

Even though it cannot be prepared or assembled the night before, we just can't resist telling you about fried garlic bread. If you like your garlic bread both crunchy and moist, and literally dripping with garlic, try this: sauté lots of minced or crushed garlic in lots of butter, dip both sides of rounds of French bread or slices of white bread in the melted garlic butter so that the bread soaks up all the butter, then fry over fairly high heat until both sides are crisp and lightly browned.

Quick Whole Wheat Bread

1¼ cups sifted white flour
2½ cups sifted whole wheat
    flour
3 tablespoons sugar
1 teaspoon baking soda

1 teaspoon salt
¼-lb. stick of butter (cold)
1 cup raisins (optional)
2 eggs
1 cup buttermilk

The Night Before

Preparation Time: 20 min.   *Cooking Time:* 50 min.

Heat oven to 400°.

Sift flours before measuring. Pour sifted flours into a large bowl. Sift in the sugar, baking soda, and salt and mix.

Blend the butter into the flour with a pastry cutter until the mixture is about the consistency of cornmeal. Add the raisins at this point if you're using them and mix well.

Beat the eggs in a separate bowl and add the buttermilk. Mix.

Make a well in the center of the flour and pour the egg-buttermilk mixture into the well. Mix into the dry ingredients with a wooden spoon.

Turn the dough out onto a floured wooden board and knead a few times into a ball. Flatten the top slightly and make 2 cuts with a sharp knife on the top of the loaf, about ½″ deep and forming an X across the top.

Place the loaf on a buttered or Teflon cookie sheet and bake for 50 minutes.

Makes 1 loaf
Can be frozen

Cheese Bread

You could cut this recipe in half and make only one loaf, but it really wouldn't be sensible. It takes about the same time to make 2 loaves and you can put one in the freezer for later use. It's an excellent bread however you serve it but it's very special toasted for meat sandwiches—the toasting brings out the cheese flavor in a way that turns a prosaic delicatessen meat sandwich into an event.

Since this bread has to have time to rise twice, make it on an evening when you can start early or are planning to stay up for the late show. Or better still, try a rainy Sunday afternoon; the smell of baking bread will do wonders for the morale of anyone within sniffing distance.

½ cup warm water
2 packages powdered yeast
½ cup sugar
1½ cups milk
1 tablespoon salt
¼ cup butter, room temperature

1 egg
2 cups grated or shredded Cheddar cheese
6 cups sifted flour
2 tablespoons melted butter

The Night Before

Preparation Time: 35 min.

Rising Time: approximately 3 hrs.
Baking Time: 30 min.

Put the ½ cup of warm water (just hot enough not to feel uncomfortable on your hand) into a small bowl. Add the yeast and 1 teaspoon of the sugar. Cover the bowl and put it in a warm corner of the kitchen for 10 minutes.

Scald the milk. Remove from the stove and add the rest of the sugar, the salt, and the butter. Stir until the butter is melted.

Pour the milk mixture into a large bowl and add the yeast mixture to it. Stir. Beat the egg and add the egg and the cheese. Mix again. Add 3 cups of the flour and mix until it leaves the side of the bowl. Add the remaining 3 cups of flour and mix again.

Lightly flour a board and put the dough on the board. Knead it for 10 minutes by pushing down hard on the side of the dough nearest you with the palms of your hands, then folding the dough over and repeating the pushing, turning the dough frequently. Sprinkle a little additional flour on the board if the dough is sticky toward the beginning of the kneading process.

Rinse out the large bowl of your electric mixer with hot water, dry it and grease the bottom and sides with butter. Put the ball of dough in the bowl and turn it around so that all sides are buttered. Cover the bowl with a damp tea towel and set in a draft-free place until the dough doubles in bulk—about 2 hours. You will know that it has risen enough if, when you poke your finger in it, the indentation stays.

When the dough has doubled, punch it down with your fist and then reshape it into a ball, kneading 2 or 3 times. Put the dough back on the board, divide it into 2 pieces, cover with the tea towel, and let it rest for 10 minutes. In the meantime, melt the butter.

Shape the bread into 2 loaves and place each loaf in a bread pan, making sure that the dough touches the edges of the pan on all 4 sides. Brush with melted butter, cover pans with the tea towel, and let the pans stand in a warm place until the dough doubles in bulk again—about 45 minutes.

Heat oven to 375° and bake bread for 30 minutes. Turn the loaves out onto a rack to cool. *2 loaves*

Can be frozen

Popovers

If you use presifted flour, a blender, and a Teflon muffin pan, which doesn't need to be greased, you can have fresh piping hot popovers with less than 5 minutes' work. If you have to sift the flour, mix by hand, or butter the muffin pan, you'll have to add a bit to the preparation time.

⅞ cup milk
2 eggs
1 tablespoon butter

1 cup sifted flour
¼ teaspoon salt

Preparation Time: 5 min.   *Cooking Time:* 40 min.

Heat oven to 425°.

Put ingredients in blender in order given. Blend for 20 to 30 seconds.

Pour batter into a 12-cup muffin tin.

Bake for 40 minutes. When you take the popovers out of the oven, make a small gash with a knife in the side of each one to let steam escape.

12 popovers

Blueberry Bread

1¼ cups fresh blueberries or 1
   15-oz. can
¼ lb. sweet butter
3 cups sifted flour
1 tablespoon baking powder
¼ teaspoon baking soda

½ cup sugar
1 teaspoon salt
3 eggs
½ cup milk
⅓ cup orange juice

The Night Before

Preparation Time: 12 min.   *Cooking Time:* 1 hr.

Rinse blueberries if you're using fresh ones or drain the canned berries thoroughly.

Melt butter.

In a large bowl, mix the sifted flour, baking powder, soda, sugar, and salt.

Beat the eggs in another bowl. Add the butter, milk, and orange juice and mix. Pour this mixture over the flour and mix with a wooden spoon just until the dry and liquid ingredients are well mixed.

Spoon the batter into a greased or Teflon loaf pan.

Heat oven to 350°. Let the batter rest for 10 to 15 minutes before placing the pan in the oven.

Bake for 1 hour. Cool pan on a rack for 10 minutes before turning the bread out.

Makes 1 loaf
Can be frozen

Oatmeal Bread

2 cups quick-cooking oats
2 tablespoons butter
2 cups sifted flour
¼ cup sugar
1 teaspoon salt

1 teaspoon baking powder
1 teaspoon baking soda
1⅔ cups milk
½ cup molasses
1 cup golden raisins

The Night Before

Preparation Time: 13 min.   *Cooking Time:* 1 hr.

Crush oats in the blender by processing at high speed for 30 seconds.

Melt butter.

Sift together into a large mixing bowl the sifted flour, sugar, salt, baking powder, and baking soda. Mix in the crushed oats.

Add the milk, melted butter, and molasses and mix well. Stir in raisins.

Pour batter into a greased or Teflon-lined loaf pan. Heat oven to 350° but let the batter stand at room temperature in the pan for 15 minutes before putting it in the oven.

Bake for 1 hour. Remove pan to a rack to cool for 10 minutes before turning the bread out. Let the bread cool completely before wrapping it for storage or freezing.

Makes 1 loaf
Can be frozen

Bread with Scallion Butter

8 scallions
16 sprigs parsley
¼ cup frozen or fresh chives

¾ cup soft margarine or
whipped butter
1 large loaf Italian bread

The Night Before

Preparation Time: 5 min.

Chop scallions fine. Mince parsley and chives. Mix scallions, parsley, and chives with soft margarine or whipped butter.

Cut Italian bread in half horizontally. Spread both halves with margarine or butter mixture and put loaf together again. Wrap in aluminum foil and refrigerate.

Before Serving

Preparation Time: 1 min.   *Cooking Time:* 15 to 20 min.

Heat oven to 350°.

Bake bread, still wrapped in foil, for 10 minutes. Remove foil and bake for another 5 or 10 minutes.

Serves 8

Section Four

ACCESSORIES BEFORE AND AFTER THE FACT

□ APPETIZERS AND SOUPS □

Mozzarella Appetizer

10 thin slices white bread	1 small can anchovy filets
¼ lb. mozzarella cheese, very thinly sliced	1 teaspoon dried oregano

The Night Before

Preparation Time: 4 min.

Toast bread slices very lightly, then trim crusts and cut each slice into triangles, rectangles, or rounds—depending on what strikes your fancy and suits the shape of your cheese. On each piece, place a slice of cheese, an anchovy, and a few flakes of oregano. Place on broiler tray, cover with plastic wrap or foil, and refrigerate.

Before Serving

Preparation Time: ½ min.   *Cooking Time:* 2 min.

Remove broiler tray from refrigerator, uncover, and broil mozzarella appetizers until cheese melts—about 2 min.

Serves 6 to 8

Gravlax with Dill Sauce

If you have a taste for Scotch smoked salmon but you've given up hope of serving it to your guests because the current price presents you with a choice between the salmon and next summer's vacation, Gravlax may be your discovery of the year. It isn't, we hasten to say, a smoked salmon; it's marinated in your refrigerator for 2 to 3 days (preferably 3) and served with a mustardy dill sauce accompanied by triangles of very, very thin pumpernickel. In Sweden it is sometimes used as a main course; we think you'll prefer it as an appetizer.

One word of warning: don't make this unless fresh dill is available. Freeze-dried or bottled dill may be an effective substitute for many dishes but it wouldn't do at all for this one.

FOR THE SALMON

2 lbs. center-cut fresh salmon, scaled and boned
1 large bunch fresh dill
¼ cup sugar
¼ cup kosher coarse salt
2 tablespoons whole peppercorns

FOR THE SAUCE

¼ cup Dijon or other strong mustard
3 tablespoons sugar
2 tablespoons vinegar
⅓ cup vegetable oil
¼ cup snipped dill

Two or Three Nights Before Serving

Preparation Time: 12 min.

Wash the dill. Snip ¼ cup and reserve it for the sauce. Cut the rest of the dill horizontally in thirds.

Crack the peppercorns with the back of a cleaver or a rolling pin. Combine them with the salt and sugar.

Place about one-third of the dill on the bottom of a casserole large enough to hold the folded salmon flat. Open the salmon out with the skin side down and place about two-thirds of the remaining dill on the bottom half of the salmon. Top with the salt-sugar-pepper mixture. Fold the top over and place the salmon in the casserole. Sprinkle the remaining dill over the top skin.

Cover the salmon with a plate just slightly smaller than the casserole or with plastic wrap, topped by aluminum foil. Refrigerate, placing heavy cans on top of the plate or foil to weigh down the salmon.

As it sits in the refrigerator the salmon will generate a liquid. Once in the morning and once at night, remove the casserole from the refrigerator, baste the inside of the salmon with the liquid, turn the salmon over, and replace it in the refrigerator with the weights. The fish is ready to be served when it has marinated for 24 to 36 hours.

To make the sauce, put the mustard, sugar, and vinegar in the small bowl of the electric mixer and mix at low speed. With the mixer running, add the oil very slowly and continue beating for about 2 minutes until the sauce is thickened. Stir in the reserved snipped dill. Cover and refrigerate.

Before Serving
Preparation Time: 10 min.

Place the fish, skin side down and opened, on a flat board and scrape off all the dill and seasonings.

With a sharp knife, cut thin diagonal slices. (Do not cut through the skin, which you will be discarding.)

Stir the dill sauce thoroughly before serving with the sliced salmon.   *Serves 8 to 10*

Dip De Luxe: Caviar and Sour Cream

While not wishing to offend the sensibilities of those caviar aficionados who feel that only the $85-per-pound stuff is worth eating, we contend that for this particular purpose the least expensive jar of caviar on your supermarket shelf will serve very well. It's the blending of flavors and textures that's important here, not the outrageously fine quality of one ingredient. The governing rule: anything that costs a dollar a taste ought to be really tasted. Don't mask its flavor by combining it with sour cream, wine, or even dinner, for that matter.

Warning: Since this dip takes so little time to prepare, you may be tempted to wait until just before serving time to put it together. Don't—it takes at least 6 to 8 hours for the flavors to blend properly.

3 to 4 tablespoons finely minced onion	2 cups (1 pint) sour cream
	4 to 6 oz. red caviar

The Night Before

Preparation Time: 5 min.

Mince onion.

Add caviar and onion to sour cream. (You can do this right in the sour cream container if you wish.) Mix well and turn into serving dish. Refrigerate until ready to serve.

Serves 8 to 10

Split Pea Soup

1 chopped onion	5 cups chicken broth
3 tablespoons butter	4 cups water
3 tomatoes	2 teaspoons salt
1 lb. yellow split peas	½ teaspoon white pepper
1 ham hock (about 2 lbs.)	2 carrots

. . . .

¾ cup heavy sweet cream	1 tablespoon butter

The Night Before

Preparation Time: 27 min. *Cooking Time:* 2 hrs., 15 min.

Chop the onion and sauté it in the butter in a large pot until tender but not brown. While it is cooking, chop the tomatoes into large dice. Add to the wilted onions and cook, stirring, for about 5 minutes.

Add all other ingredients above the dotted line (except the carrots) to the pot. Cook over medium heat for 2 hours.

Pare the carrots and cut into thin slices. Cut each slice into julienne strips. Drop strips into boiling water and cook for 10 minutes. Drain, cover, and refrigerate.

Remove the pot from the stove and allow the soup to cool a bit. Remove and discard ham hock.

When soup is cool, put it through the blender at high speed, a little at a time. Refrigerate.

Before Serving

Preparation Time: 2 min.   *Cooking Time:* 5 min.

Heat the soup for a few minutes. Add the cream and bring to the boiling point.

Add the carrot strips and the butter and stir until the butter is melted.

Serves 10
Can be frozen

Curried Crabmeat Spread

7- or 8-oz. can crabmeat
1 large apple
1 stalk celery
1 cup raisins

1 cup mayonnaise
1 teaspoon (or more) curry powder

The Night Before

Preparation Time: 7 min.

Flake crabmeat, removing any bits of bone and cartilage. Core and dice apple, mince celery.

Place all ingredients in small bowl and mix well. Taste for seasoning and add more curry powder if necessary. Cover and refrigerate.

Before Serving

Preparation Time: 1 min.

Arrange on serving dish with sesame seed crackers. *Serves 8*

Vegetable Soup

This is a very hearty—and delicious—soup. If you're planning to use it as the main course, make it with the meatballs. If you plan it as the first but not the main course of a meal, omit the meatballs.

1 carrot	1 teaspoon oregano
3 stalks celery, with leaves	½ cup small pasta or noodle flakes
1 can (1-lb.) Italian tomatoes	
6 cups canned beef broth	

FOR MEATBALLS

2 slices toast	1 egg
½ cup water	1 clove garlic
1 lb. chopped chuck	1 teaspoon salt

. . . .

grated Parmesan cheesee

The Night Before

Preparation Time: 12 min. for soup only or 20 min. with meatballs.

Cooking Time: 25 min.

SOUP

Peel and coarsely cube the carrot and cut the celery in chunks. Blend, using the canned tomatoes and some of the beef broth as your liquid in the blending process.

Pour all the beef broth and the blended vegetables, tomatoes, and oregano into a pot and bring to a boil. Cover and simmer for 10 minutes.

Add the pasta or noodle flakes and simmer for an additional 10 minutes.

Cover and refrigerate.

MEATBALLS

Soak the toast in water and squeeze dry. Mince the garlic. Toss the toast lightly with the beef, beaten egg, minced garlic, and salt. Shape into small meatballs, one inch in diameter.

Bake in 350° oven for 20 minutes.

Refrigerate separately in a covered bowl.

Before Serving

Preparation Time: 1 min.　　　　　　　　*Cooking Time:* 10 min.

Add meatballs to soup and simmer for 10 minutes until hot.

Serve with grated Parmesan cheese.　　　　　　*Serves 6*

Chopped Liver

1 lb. beef (or calf or chicken) liver

2 medium onions

2 eggs, hard boiled

6 tablespoons chicken fat or mayonnaise

1 teaspoon salt

⅛ teaspoon pepper

The Night Before

Preparation Time: 15 min.　　　　　*Cooking Time:* 10 to 12 min.

Cut liver into 2- to 3-inch chunks. Place in pot with water to cover and cook until centers of liver chunks are no longer pink—this will take 10 to 12 min. While the liver is cooking, hard-boil 2 eggs and peel the onions and cut them in chunks.

Put liver, onions, and eggs through the fine blade of your food grinder. If you are using chicken fat, melt it in a small skillet before adding it to the liver. Add the chicken fat or mayonnaise and the salt and pepper to the liver mixture and mix well.

Before Serving

Preparation Time: 3 min.

To serve as an appetizer, for each portion put a mound of chopped liver on a couple of lettuce leaves and garnish with a sprig of parsley. This can also be served with crackers as a cocktail spread.　　　　　*Serves 6* as an appetizer

Serves 12 as a cocktail spread

Cheese Ball

4 oz. Roquefort cheese
8 oz. Cheddar cheese, grated or shredded
6 oz. (2 small packages) cream cheese
1 onion, finely minced

1 teaspoon Worcestershire sauce
½ cup chopped walnuts
3 tablespoons chopped chives or parsley (optional)

The Night Before

Preparation Time: 12 min.

Allow the cheeses to stand at room temperature until they soften. Combine them with onion and Worcestershire. Refrigerate for about an hour, until firm enough to mold into a ball. Roll the cheese ball in chopped walnuts and, if you wish, chopped chives or parsley. Wrap in waxed paper and refrigerate.

Before Serving

Let stand at room temperature for 10 min. Serve with crackers or dark bread. The uneaten portion of the cheese ball is easily salvaged: mold it back into a ball, reroll in chopped walnuts, wrap, and freeze. It will keep beautifully in the freezer.

Serves 8

Green Pea Soup (with a French twist)

If you're feeling ambitious about shelling peas, you can make this with 3 cups of fresh peas (about 2¼ lbs.), but, if you do, add 1 teaspoon of sugar when you cook the peas and increase the cooking time in Step 2 to 15 minutes after boiling.

It's really worth making with fresh peas. It will take about 25 minutes to shell the peas—just time to hear your favorite record or watch a half-hour television show. But this time is hypothetical. Shelling peas is an irresistible occupation and anyone in your vicinity is likely to pitch in and make you feel like Tom Sawyer and the whitewash job.

½ head of lettuce, shredded
15 spinach leaves, shredded
¾ cup green part of scallions or leaks, sliced
2 10-oz. packages frozen green peas, thawed (or 3 cups fresh, shelled peas)

7 sprigs parsley
4 tablespoons butter
1 teaspoon salt
½ teaspoon white pepper
4 cups chicken stock (or 2 cans condensed chicken broth plus 1 can of water)

. . . .

6 tablespoons heavy sweet cream

3 tablespoons butter

The Night Before

Preparation Time: 20 min.   *Cooking Time:* 20 min.

Wash and pat dry the lettuce leaves and spinach. Shred. Chop leek or scallion tops, saving the bulb part for another use.

Reserve 2½ cups of the chicken stock. Put all other above-the-line ingredients in a large pot and bring to a boil. Reduce heat, cover, and simmer for 10 minutes.

Put the soup, about a third at a time, through the blender at medium speed, blending for about 45 seconds for each batch.

Return the purée to the pot, stir in the remaining chicken stock, and bring to a boil, stirring occasionally.

Cool, cover, and refrigerate the pot.

Before Serving

Preparation Time: 3 min.   *Cooking Time:* 12 min.

Reheat soup over a medium flame until it is hot but not boiling.

Add cream and butter gradually, stirring continuously until butter is all melted.
                                                  Serves 6
                                              Can be frozen

Chinese Roast Pork

The secret of this oriental pork is that it's cooked hanging up, not lying down. If that sounds difficult to do in a standard American oven, don't panic; it can be done very easily. All that you do is supply yourself with a few drapery hooks, remove all the shelves from your oven except the very top one and place a roasting pan lined with aluminum foil and filled with about an inch of cold water at the bottom of the oven. Then put a hook through the end of each pork strip, hook the other end of the hook over the steel rod of your top oven shelf and there you are! The cooked pork can be wrapped in aluminum foil and refrigerated or frozen and then reheated in the same aluminum foil when you're ready to use it. It makes a fine appetizer and a great sandwich if you have any left.

2 lbs. pork fillets or lean pork tenderloin
1 slice fresh ginger root
½ cup soy sauce
¼ cup sherry
1 tablespoon brown sugar
1 tablespoon honey
2 teaspoons red food coloring

The Night Before

Preparation Time: 10 min.   *Cooking Time:* 55 min.

Cut the pork into strips about 2 inches in diameter and 4 inches long (or longer if your oven rack is high enough so that they won't trail in the water in the roasting pan at the bottom of the oven).

Mince the ginger and mix it into a marinade made by combining all the remaining ingredients. Marinate the pork in this mixture for 2 hours at room temperature, turning the strips once in a while.

Before lighting the oven, place the roasting pan on the bottom shelf of the oven and hang the pork strips as described in the note above. Discard the marinade.

Heat oven to 375° and bake pork for 55 minutes.

Wrap pork strips in aluminum foil and refrigerate.

Preparation Time: 4 min.   *Cooking Time:* 20 min.

Heat oven to 350°. Place pork, still wrapped in foil, in a pan and heat for 20 minutes.

Slice and serve.

Serves 8
Can be frozen

Chicken Egg Drop Soup

2 scallions (green onions), with their green tops, chopped

. . . .

4 cups chicken broth (or 2 cans [14 oz.] uncondensed chicken soup or 2 cans of condensed chicken soup plus one can of water)	¼ teaspoon sugar
	½ teaspoon salt
	⅛ teaspoon pepper
	1 egg, beaten
	¼ cup cold water
1½ tablespoons cornstarch	

The Night Before

Preparation Time: 2 min.

Wash and chop scallions and store in refrigerator in waxed paper or plastic bag.

Before Serving

Preparation Time: 3 min.   *Cooking Time:* 7 min.

Heat broth to boiling point. Meanwhile, beat the egg in one small dish or glass. In another, make a smooth paste of the cornstarch and cold water; then add the sugar, salt, and pepper to the cornstarch mixture.

When the soup has boiled, pour the cornstarch mixture slowly into it, stirring constantly. Allow the soup to reach the boiling point again. Cook and stir for 1 min. until soup is thick and translucent. Then add the beaten egg, very slowly, stirring constantly. When all the egg has been added, remove the soup from the stove, pour into tureen or serving dish and sprinkle scallions over top.

Serves 4

Vichysoisse

This recipe uses only the white part of the leeks. The Green Pea Soup on page 224 uses the green part. You may decide to make both soups the same week and use all the leeks economically. If you do, you can freeze part or all of the green pea soup for future use.

This potato soup can also be served hot. If this is the way you're going to use it, you can stop after Step 5 and add the milk and cream when you reheat the soup just before serving.

2 leeks, white part only	2 teaspoons salt
1 small onion	⅛ teaspoon white pepper
2 tablespoons butter	1 cup milk
3 potatoes (about 1¼ lbs.)	¾ cup heavy sweet cream
2½ cups chicken broth	

. . . .

2 tablespoons snipped fresh   or freeze-dried chives

The Night Before
Preparation Time: 25 min.   *Cooking Time:* 35 min.

Slice leeks and onion.

Melt butter in a saucepan and cook the leeks and onion over a very low flame until barely wilted but not browned.

Peel and slice potato thin.

Add sliced potatoes, chicken broth, salt, and white pepper to the pan. Bring to a boil, then lower heat and simmer gently for 20 minutes, until potatoes are soft.

Put the potato mixture through the blender, part at a time, pouring the blended soup into a clean pan.

Add milk and cream and heat soup until just below the boiling point, stirring frequently.

Refrigerate the soup, covered.

Before Serving
Preparation Time: 2 min.

Put the soup through the blender again or stir it thoroughly

before serving. Sprinkle chives on top of each portion.
See also Cabbage Soup, page 155.

Serves 4
Can be frozen

Chicken Soup with Matzo Balls (Knadlaick)

2½ tablespoons chicken fat (or butter if you must)
2 large or 3 medium eggs
¼ cup water or club soda

1 teaspoon salt
¼ teaspoon white pepper
¾ cup matzo meal

. . . .

6 cups chicken broth (or 3 14-oz. cans uncondensed chicken broth or 3 cans condensed chicken broth plus 2 cans water)

The Night Before

Preparation Time: 3 min.

Put the chicken fat or butter in the small bowl of your electric mixer. Beat at medium speed until creamy. Add eggs and beat again.

Add the water, salt, pepper, and matzo meal and beat again. Cover bowl and refrigerate.

Before Serving

Preparation Time: 4 min.   *Cooking Time:* 30 min.

Boil about 2 quarts water in a fairly wide saucepan. While it is boiling, wet your hands with cold water and shape the matzo meal batter into small balls about the size of a walnut.

When the water boils, add salt and drop the matzo balls gently into the water. Reduce heat, cover, and simmer for 30 minutes.

Heat the chicken broth during the last 10 minutes of the cooking time for the matzo balls.

Remove the matzo balls with a slotted spoon and add to each bowl of soup.

Serves 6

Blender Gazpacho

This cold Spanish vegetable soup is a fine beginning for a warm weather meal. It's also high in nourishment and low in calories. A jar of gazpacho in the refrigerator is a satisfying substitute for some less virtuous snacking.

3 tomatoes	4 eggs
1 medium onion	¼ cup vinegar
1 cucumber	¾ cup tomato juice
2 cloves garlic	¼ teaspoon salt
1 green pepper	¼ teaspoon cayenne

. . . .

croutons (optional)

The Night Before

Preparation Time: 20 min.

Remove stems from tomatoes and drop them into boiling water for 1 minute. Remove with a long fork and hold the tomatoes under cold running water to cool. This will enable you to slip the peels off easily.

Peel the onion, cucumber, and garlic. Remove the stem and seeds of the pepper and rinse and dry it. Cut the vegetables into whatever size pieces are necessary for your particular blender.

Blend tomatoes and garlic. Add onion and blend again. Add green pepper and blend. Add cucumber and blend once more. Pour contents of blender into a bowl.

Put the eggs, vinegar, tomato juice, salt, and cayenne into the blender. Blend for half a minute, then pour the egg mixture into the bowl with the vegetable purée. Mix.

Being careful not to overload your blender, put the soup back into the blender, part at a time, and reblend. Cover and refrigerate.

Before Serving

Preparation Time: 1 min.

Pour soup into bowls. Add croutons if desired. *Serves 6*

Salmon Mousse

This is easy, decorative, and delicious. Our talented friend, Marion Brown, once doubled the recipe, made it in a copper fish mold and decorated it with olive slices for the eyes, strips of pimiento for scales. It was the sensation of a large buffet—so beautiful that until the hostess ruthlessly cut into it, nobody wanted to desecrate her work of art. For simpler service, you can pour this into a small loaf pan and serve it in slices, a small bowl and serve it in wedges, or individual little porcelain casseroles.

1-lb. can salmon
½ cup boiling water
1 envelope unflavored gelatin
2 tablespoons lemon juice
1 small slice onion

½ cup mayonnaise
½ teaspoon paprika
½ teaspoon dried dill (or 1 tablespoon fresh)
1 cup heavy sweet cream

The Night Before

Preparation Time: 6 min.

Turn the salmon out onto a plate so you can find and discard the bones and dark skin.

Put into the container of the blender the ½ cup of boiling water, the gelatin, lemon juice, and onion. Blend at medium speed.

Add to the blender the mayonnaise, salmon, paprika, and dill. Blend at high speed.

Reduce the blender speed to low and, with the blender running, add the cream gradually.

Pour into a mold, pan, or bowl or directly into individual small serving dishes; cover and refrigerate.

Before Serving

Preparation Time: 1 to 3 min.

If the mousse is not already in individual serving dishes, unmold it from the pan or bowl in which it was refrigerated; cut into serving pieces if you're not planning to serve it whole.

Serves 8

Guacamole

1 tomato, peeled and finely chopped
1 green pepper, finely chopped
3 tablespoons grated onion
2 large ripe avocados
2 teaspoons lime juice

1 teaspoon olive oil
1½ teaspoons chili powder
¼ teaspoon salt, plus more to taste
⅛ teaspoon black pepper
mayonnaise

The Night Before

Preparation Time: 11 min.

Peel and chop tomato. (Tomato can be peeled easily if you drop it in boiling water for half a minute and then run cold water over it.) Seed and chop green pepper. Grate onion. Set aside.

Mash avocados (they must be ripe) and immediately add lime juice. Add vegetables and all other ingredients except mayonnaise. Taste and add more salt and/or pepper, according to taste.

Place in a jar or other deep container that is about 3 or 4 inches in diameter. Cover surface with a thick layer of mayonnaise—this will prevent discoloration. Cover container securely with its own tight-fitting cover or with plastic wrap and a rubber band.

Before Serving

Preparation Time: 1 min.

Mix mayonnaise into the Guacamole.

Serve as a first course or salad by piling on lettuce leaves arranged on individual plates; or serve as a dip to accompany pre-dinner cocktails by heaping into a bowl and surrounding with potato or corn chips.

Serves 4 as a salad or first course
Serves 8 to 10 as a dip

Taramsalata

You can, if you like, use this as a kind of super-dip. It is really a Greek appetizer which should be served with French or Italian bread or, if it is available in your area, pitta—flat Arab bread.

If you have trouble finding salted fish roe, you can substitute inexpensive red caviar very successfully.

4 slices white bread	4 oz. tarama (salted fish roe)
1 cup milk	¼ cup lemon juice
3 tablespoons finely chopped onion	¼ cup olive oil
	½ cup vegetable oil

The Night Before

Preparation Time: 20 min.

Trim and discard crusts from bread. Put bread in a bowl, pour the milk over it, and allow it to soak for 5 minutes while you chop the onion.

Squeeze the bread dry and put it in the small bowl of your electric mixer. Beat at medium speed until it is a smooth paste.

Add the fish roe or caviar, a tablespoon at a time, beating constantly. Add lemon juice.

Mix the two oils together and add, a tablespoon at a time, beating between each addition until you have added half the oil. With the mixer going, add the rest of the oil in a slow steady stream. Beat until the mixture is fluffy and pink. Add the onion and beat again.

Refrigerate, covered.

Before Serving

Preparation Time: 1 min.

Place each portion on a lettuce leaf and serve.   *Serves 6*

Marinated Shrimp

The preparation time does not include shelling and deveining shrimp. See page 96.

2 lbs. shrimp	½ teaspoon chili powder
2 onions, diced	¼ teaspoon dry mustard
2 large onions, sliced in thin rings	1½ teaspoons salt
	½ teaspoon black pepper
3 split cloves garlic	½ cup vinegar
¾ cup olive oil	

The Night Before

Preparation and Cooking Time: 25 min.

Shell and devein shrimp. Dry on paper towels.

Dice and peel onions and peel garlic.

Sauté the chopped onions and garlic in ¼ cup olive oil for 10 minutes. Add the shrimp and sauté for 7 or 8 minutes, stirring a few times during cooking. Remove shrimp from pan with a slotted spoon and set aside to cool while you prepare sauce.

Mix the remaining ½ cup olive oil together with all the other ingredients listed. Add the shrimp, being sure to coat all the shrimp with the marinade.

Cover the dish and refrigerate. Baste the shrimp whenever you have to go to the refrigerator later in the evening or the next morning.

Before Serving

Serve cold.

Serves 8 as an appetizer or 20 to 25 as an hors d'oeuvre

Ham Mousse

While we use this as an appetizer, you could double the recipe and use it as the base for a main course luncheon dish. In either case, it's a fine way to use up leftover ham or to take advantage of a sale on boiled ham at your market.

½ lb. cooked ham	3 tablespoons mayonnaise
2 tablespoons butter (room temperature)	1 tablespoon port
	⅛ teaspoon cayenne

. . . .

4 canned pear halves

The Night Before
Preparation Time: 5 min.

Cut the ham into small pieces and process in the blender, adding a little at a time.

Turn the ham into the small bowl of your electric mixer. Add the softened butter, mayonnaise, wine, and cayenne and beat at medium speed until well mixed.

Cover bowl and refrigerate.

Before Serving
Preparation Time: 5 min.

Drain the pear halves and pat dry with paper towel.

Heap some of the ham mousse in each pear half.   *Serves 4*

Greek Cheese Pies

Admittedly, these hors d'oeuvres are slightly complicated and time-consuming to prepare, and take up a good deal of your counter space while you're at it. However, they are absolutely delicious and freeze beautifully. Once you invest the hour or so required, you can tuck whatever you're not using immediately away in the freezer to save for unexpected guests or your next party.

Phyllo dough is sold frozen at gourmet, Greek, and Middle Eastern food shops and many cheese stores. If you cannot find it you may substitute strudel dough if that is available.

1¼ lbs. feta cheese	½ teaspoon pepper
3 eggs	3 tablespoons minced fresh par-
2 egg yolks	sley (optional)
2½ cups milk	1-lb. package of phyllo sheets
5 tablespoons butter	¾ cup butter
5 tablespoons flour	¾ cup olive oil

The Night Before
Preparation Time: 1 hr., 15 min.

Crumble feta cheese into large bowl and set aside.

Break the eggs and egg yolks into a small bowl and set aside.

Heat milk in small saucepan. Meanwhile, in a large saucepan, melt butter, add flour, stir with wire whisk and cook for one minute. Add hot milk to butter-flour mixture and beat with wire whisk to blend well.

Add ¼ cup of the butter-flour-milk mixture to the eggs and mix with fork. Then slowly add eggs to saucepan containing milk mixture; stir constantly with a wire whisk as you add the eggs. Cook and stir over medium heat until sauce is very thick —about 5 minutes. Remove from heat and pour into bowl of feta cheese. Add pepper and minced parsley and mix thoroughly.

Melt butter and olive oil together in small saucepan and either keep warm over low heat or remove from heat and set aside.

Unwrap phyllo dough and place it in front of you on a large cutting board. Cut into strips by dividing into 5 equal parts and cutting through all layers as shown.

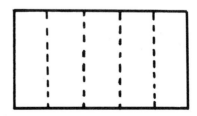

Place as many single strips of phyllo on your cutting board as it has room for. Keep the rest of them covered with plastic wrap or foil to prevent them from drying out. Brush each strip with melted butter and olive oil. Place a teaspoonful of feta cheese mixture about one inch from the bottom of each strip. Roll the strips into triangles as illustrated:

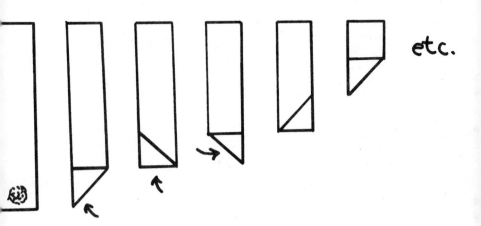

etc.

Place triangles on a baking sheet and brush with butter-olive oil mixture. Repeat until all strips are used—you will need several baking sheets.

Cover baking sheets with aluminum foil and refrigerate or freeze. (If you are freezing the pastries for later use, you may remove them from the baking sheets after they are solidly frozen and store them in another container.)

Before Serving

Cooking Time: 12 to 15 min.
(15 to 20 min. if frozen)

Preheat oven to 400°.
Bake until pastry is crisp and lightly browned.

Makes 100 pieces
Can be frozen

Seviche

If the thought of eating uncooked fish upsets you, think of smoked salmon or pickled herring and be reassured that these scallops do not taste raw. Seviche is good as a first course and is also a good addition to the hors d'oeuvres tray.

6 limes (or enough to produce
   ¾ cup juice)
¾ lb. scallops
1 onion

3 sprigs parsley
1 small green pepper
1 tomato
⅓ cup olive oil

. . . .

salt and pepper

The Night Before
Preparation Time: 15 min.

Squeeze enough limes to produce ¾ cup juice. Pour lime juice over scallops in dish. Cover and refrigerate.

Slice onion into thin rings. Mince parsley. Chop green pepper. Plunge tomato into boiling water for a minute, then hold under cold running water. Now peel and chop tomato.

Put onion, parsley, tomato, green pepper, and olive oil into container. Cover and refrigerate.

Before Serving
Preparation Time: 2 min.

Drain lime juice from scallops and place them in a serving dish. Pour the olive-oil vegetable mixture over scallops. Add salt and freshly ground pepper (or cracked pepper) to taste.

Serves 6 as a first course

Stracciatella

While the directions below let you prepare the night before, we confess that this rather interesting Italian chicken soup is one that we normally make just before dinner time. That's because it uses ingredients you're likely to have on your pantry shelf and in your refrigerator at the moment you learn you're going to be feeding more people at dinner than you had planned. Adding a soup course is a sure-fire way of making the dinner you planned for 4 stretch to serve 6.

3 eggs	¼ cup grated Parmesan cheese
1 tablespoon cold water	2 tablespoons minced parsley

. . . .

6 cups chicken broth

The Night Before
Preparation Time: 5 min.

Beat eggs and water together in a small bowl or jar. Add cheese and parsley.

Cover and refrigerate.

Before Serving
Preparation Time: 2 min.   *Cooking Time:* 10 min.

Bring chicken broth to a boil.

Restir the egg mixture. When soup boils, pour the egg mixture into the soup very slowly, stirring the soup with a fork until the egg sets.   *Serves 6 to 8*

Three-Way Eggplant

This dish acquired its name because it has at various times appeared on our tables serving three different functions. It is an excellent canapé spread on tiny slices of rye bread or dark pumpernickel. Or it can appear as a scoop of eggplant on a lettuce leaf as a first course. Last, but not least, it can be served as an excellent cold vegetable for a night when you don't want to be bothered making a salad. It can be made at any convenient time and kept in the refrigerator for a week—provided that you lock the refrigerator.

1 medium eggplant
¼ cup minced onion
2 tablespoons olive oil
¼ cup lemon juice

1½ teaspoons salt
1 teaspoon sugar
⅛ teaspoon pepper

The Night Before

Preparation Time: 15 min.   *Cooking Time:* 15 min.

Heat oven to 475°. While it is heating, squeeze lemons and chop onion. Bake eggplant for about 15 min. or until skin turns dark brown. Cool and peel.

If you have a blender, blend cubes of eggplant together with rest of ingredients. If you have no blender, chop the eggplant fine and then stir in other ingredients. Refrigerate.

Before Serving

Preparation Time: 1 min.

Pour off any excess liquid and serve.

Serves 5 to 6 as an appetizer or vegetable
Serves 12 to 20 as an hors d'oeuvre

Marinated Chicken Wings

3 lbs. (about 15) chicken wings
½ cup soy sauce

½ cup honey
¼ cup lemon juice

The Night Before

Preparation Time: 5 min. (20 min. if wings are whole)

If you must prepare the chicken wings yourself (most butchers will do this for good customers), cut the wing tips off and either discard them or save them for the soup pot, then cut each wing at the joint to form 2 pieces.

Place the chicken wings in a large (9″ x 13″) baking pan.

Mix the soy sauce, honey, and lemon juice together and pour over the chicken wings, mixing to make sure each piece is coated with the marinade.

Cover and refrigerate.

Preheat oven to 450°.

Arrange the chicken wings skin side up and spoon some of the marinade over them.

Bake 15 minutes. If a crisper skin is desired, broil for a minute or two at the end of the baking time.   *Serves 8 to 10*
Can be frozen

Shrimp Remoulade

6 anchovies, finely chopped
2 tablespoons parsley, minced
1 scallion, diced
1 clove garlic, minced
1½ lbs. cooked cleaned shrimp (2 lbs. if you're starting with raw shrimp in the shell. See note on page 96.)

¾ cup oil, half olive oil and half vegetable oil
¼ cup tarragon vinegar
¼ cup hot mustard
3 tablespoons white horseradish
¼ teaspoon dried tarragon
¼ teaspoon white pepper
dash of Tabasco sauce

. . . .

¼ head of lettuce, shredded

The Night Before
Preparation Time: 15 min.

Chop anchovies, parsley, scallion, and garlic.

Mix all ingredients except shrimp in a small bowl.

Pour the sauce over the shrimp and mix well. Refrigerate, covered. Stir once before retiring and once again in the morning.

Before Serving
Preparation Time: 5 min.

Remove shrimp mixture from refrigerator at least half an hour before serving. The dish should be served at room temperature.

Shred lettuce. Serve shrimp and sauce over a bed of shredded lettuce.   *Serves 6 as appetizer or 4 as main course*

Shrimp Toast

½ lb. raw shrimp, shelled and deveined
½ medium onion
⅛ teaspoon ground ginger
½ teaspoon salt

Dash of black pepper
1 egg white
6 slices white bread, stale or dried in oven
½ cup fine dry bread crumbs

· · · · · · · · · · · · · ·

½ cup salad oil

The Night Before
Preparation Time: 15 min.

(*Note:* It is assumed that the shrimp have been shelled and deveined at the fish market.)

Put onions and shrimp through food grinder, using medium blade. If you do not have a food grinder, mince them with a sharp knife. Add ginger, salt, and pepper. Beat egg white lightly with a fork, then combine it with the shrimp mixture.

Remove crusts from slices of bread and cut each slice diagonally so that you have two triangles. Spread shrimp mixture on bread triangles. Heap bread crumbs on top, gently patting them down with your hands. Place on a large platter, cover with aluminum foil, and refrigerate.

Before Serving
Preparation and Cooking Time: 4 min.

Heat oil until very hot (400° in an electric skillet) and fry shrimp toast for 1 min. on each side. Drain on paper towels and serve.

Serves 6

☐ DESSERTS ☐

We have one thing in common and one difference of opinion on the subject of desserts. What we do have in common is that neither of us will admit to having tasted one in years. (We really don't know *where* those extra pounds come from!) We differ on how often dessert shows up on our menus. For one of us who had a child who in his youth had a weight problem, fresh fruit and cheese is the normal dessert with rich goodies being reserved for company dinners and special occasions. For the other mother of skinny kids, a proper dessert in that household is either sweet and gooey or sweet and crunchy—or chocolate.

The night-before cook has an almost unlimited choice of desserts that can be prepared in advance without benefit of special techniques or recipes. For that reason, we have not attempted to provide an exhaustive chapter on desserts but rather to include just a few that we especially like. How often you use them is between you and the family scale.

Pecan Pie

6 tablespoons butter
3 eggs
⅔ cup sugar
1 cup dark corn syrup

1 cup pecan halves
1 unbaked 9″ pie shell
   (preparation time is based
   on use of frozen pie shell)

The Night Before

Preparation Time: 5 min.   *Cooking Time:* 45 min.

Preheat oven to 375°.

Melt butter in small saucepan. Put melted butter, eggs, sugar, and corn syrup in mixing bowl and beat until smooth and well blended. Stir in pecan halves. Turn into pie shell.

Bake for 45 minutes. Do not refrigerate.

Serve with ice cream or, if you have time to prepare it before serving, fresh whipped cream flavored with vanilla.   *Serves 6*

Cream Puffs

For some reason, people are inordinately impressed by cream puffs, which take less time and effort to prepare than the average batch of cookies. While this recipe calls for serving them with ice cream and butterscotch sauce, you may also use pastry cream (page 254) for the filling and top them with chocolate sauce or frosting.

1 cup flour	½ cup butter
1 tablespoon sugar	4 eggs, at room temperature
1 cup water	

ice cream	1½ cups butterscotch sauce (page 252)

The Night Before

Preparation Time: 13 min.   *Cooking Time:* 45 min.

Heat oven to 425°.

Sift flour and sugar together.

Put water and butter in a large saucepan and bring to a boil. Add all of the flour (not gradually—just pour all the flour in at one time) and stir briskly until the mixture pulls away from the sides of the pan and forms a ball in the center. Remove from heat.

Add one egg and beat with a spoon until the mixture is smooth and the egg thoroughly incorporated. Repeat until all eggs are used.

Using a soup spoon as a measure, drop rounded spoonfuls of dough onto a nonstick (or greased) baking sheet, about 2 inches apart.

Bake at 425° for 15 minutes, then lower heat to 350° and bake 30 minutes longer.

Cool completely and cover. If you are going to freeze cream puffs, cut them in half first.

Preparation Time: 4 min.

Warm butterscotch sauce.

Cut the cream puffs in half. Place a scoop of ice cream on each bottom half and replace the tops. Place on dessert plates.

Spoon some butterscotch sauce on each cream puff.

Serves 8 to 10
Can be frozen

Chocolate Fudge Pie

3 squares (3 oz.) unsweetened chocolate
¾ cup butter or margarine
3 eggs

1½ cups sugar
¾ cup flour
2 teaspoons vanilla

. . . .

6 large or 8 small scoops coffee, chocolate, or vanilla ice cream

. *The Night Before*

Preparation Time: 10 min.   *Cooking Time:* 35 min.

Grease a 9″ pie pan. Heat oven to 325°.

Melt chocolate and butter (or margarine) together over very low heat, stirring often. Remove from heat and set aside.

Beat eggs until very thick and lemon-colored. Add sugar and beat for three minutes longer. Add flour and beat just long enough to blend. Stir in chocolate-butter mixture and vanilla.

Pour into greased pie pan. Bake for 35 minutes; remove from oven and let cool completely before covering the pie pan.

Before Serving

Preparation Time: 5 min.

Arrange scoops of ice cream on top of fudge pie before slicing and serving.

Serves 6 to 8

Fresh Peach Cake

6 peaches	1 egg
1 cup flour	½ teaspoon vanilla
3 tablespoons sugar	½ cup sugar
1 teaspoon baking powder	1½ teaspoons cinnamon
2 tablespoons butter	2 tablespoons butter
⅓ cup milk	

The Night Before

Preparation Time: 18 min.   *Cooking Time:* 30 min.

Grease and lightly flour a 9″ square baking pan. Heat oven to 425°. Pare and slice peaches. Set aside. Note: If you have no esthetic objection to the sight of cooked peach skins, you can save some time by not paring the peaches. If you decide to pare them, you can do so easily by dropping the peaches in boiling water for 30 seconds and then running cold water over them. The skins can then be easily removed.

Sift flour, 3 tablespoons sugar, and baking powder together into small bowl.

Cut two tablespoons butter into flour mixture with pastry blender or two knives until mixture is crumbly.

Lightly beat milk, egg, and vanilla together with a fork. Add to flour mixture and knead until well mixed. Spread dough more or less evenly into pan with a spatula.

Arrange sliced peaches on top of dough in rows or concentric circles or whatever pattern pleases you.

Mix cinnamon and ½ cup sugar together and sprinkle over peaches. Dot with two tablespoons of butter cut into small pieces. Bake for 30 minutes.

Before Serving

While this is very good served cold or at room temperature, if you can afford the time and the calories, warm the cake and serve it with freshly whipped cream.

Serves 6

Strawberry Tart

Although this recipe calls for a press-in pie shell that we like because it does not have to be rolled out, it works equally well with conventional pie crusts—homemade or frozen. Both the pie shell and the pastry cream (page 254) should be prepared an hour or two before final assembly of the tart and left to cool.

1 cup pastry cream (page 254)	½ cup butter
1 cup flour	1½ pints strawberries
¼ cup confectioner's sugar	¾ cup apricot preserves

Preparation Time: 25 min.   *Cooking Time:* 12 min.

Prepare pastry cream. Set aside to cool.

Toss flour and confectioner's sugar together in bowl. Cut butter into flour with pastry blender or two knives until mixture is crumbly. Knead dough together with your hands and roll it into a ball. Cover dough with plastic wrap and refrigerate for 30 minutes. (If you are using a frozen pie crust, eliminate this step and simply bake according to package directions.)

Hull strawberries; wash, dry, and set aside. Heat oven to 425°.

After half an hour, remove pastry dough from refrigerator and press in a 9" tart pan (a pie pan will do) forming the shell with your fingertips. Bake for 12 minutes, remove from oven and let cool.

Heat apricot preserves in a small saucepan until liquefied. Let cool.

To assemble the tart: Spread pastry cream over bottom of pie shell. Arrange strawberries, pointed side up, on top in a circular pattern. Spoon apricot glaze over strawberries. Cover with plastic wrap and store in refrigerator.   *Serves 6*

Poached Pears with Custard Sauce

4 fresh pears	¼ teaspoon cinnamon
½ cup sugar	½ teaspoon vanilla
1 cup water	6 egg yolks

. . . .

½ cup sugar	½ cup Marsala or sherry

The Night Before

Preparation Time: 16 min.   *Cooking Time:* 10 to 30 min.

Peel pears and slice in half lengthwise. Remove cores and pits.

Mix sugar, water, cinnamon, and vanilla together in a skillet large enough to hold the pears. Bring to a boil, stirring to prevent scorching. Lower heat and add pears. Simmer pears, turning halfway through cooking time, for 10 to 30 minutes. The cooking time will depend upon the texture of the pears you started with—some are softer than others. When done, the pears should be tender but not so soft that they fall apart. Cool, cover, and refrigerate.

Separate eggs. Place egg yolks in container, cover with ½″ water, and place covered container in refrigerator.

Before Serving

Preparation and Cooking Time: 12 min.

Pour water off egg yolks. Place egg yolks, ½ cup sugar, and Marsala or sherry in top of double boiler. Beat with a wire whisk.

Place over boiling water (or on lowest heat setting of electric stove) and cook, stirring constantly, until sauce becomes frothy and begins to thicken. Remove from heat and cool slightly.

Drain pears and place on dessert plates. Pour warm custard sauce over pears.

Serves 4 to 6

Trifle

Trifle is an English dessert and is one of those sweet, creamy concoctions, like a banana split, beloved by children of all ages. It is traditionally served in a glass bowl; you might use anything from a parfait glass for one serving to a punch bowl for a party-sized trifle. The quantities given below are merely a guide for assembling a trifle in a deep 2-quart bowl—you may use more or less of any ingredient and it will still taste good.

2 cups pastry cream (page 254)
6 peaches
2 tablespoons lemon juice
20 ladyfingers or 6 to 8 slices stale sponge cake
½ cup sherry

1 cup raspberry preserves
¾ cup heavy cream
1 tablespoon sugar
1 teaspoon vanilla
sliced almonds for garnish

The Night Before

Preparation Time: 20 min.

Prepare pastry cream (page 254) and let cool.

Pare and slice peaches. Sprinkle with lemon juice to keep from darkening. (Canned peaches may be substituted if fresh ones are unavailable.)

Split ladyfingers or cut sponge cake into cubes. Arrange one layer of ladyfingers or sponge cake on bottom of glass bowl. Sprinkle with some of the sherry. Place a layer of peaches over cake and a few spoonsful of raspberry preserves over peaches. Spread pastry cream over preserves. Starting again with ladyfingers or sponge cake, repeat layering until all ingredients are used.

Whip cream with sugar and vanilla. Spoon on top of trifle. Garnish with sliced almonds. Cover and refrigerate.

Serves 8 to 10

Lemon Loaf Cake

This is a firm-textured, moist cake and is best served in thin slices. For a more elaborate dessert serve it with sherbet or a fruit compote.

1 or 2 lemons	1 cup plus 6 tablespoons sugar
2 cups flour	2 eggs
1½ teaspoons baking powder	⅓ cup milk
½ cup butter	

The Night Before

Preparation Time: 15 min.   *Cooking Time:* 1 hr.

Heat oven to 350°. Grease and lightly flour a standard loaf pan.

Grate enough lemon peel to make 2 tablespoonfuls. Squeeze lemon until you have ¼ cup juice. Set aside.

Sift flour and baking powder together. Set aside.

Cream butter and one cup of the sugar with electric mixer. Add one egg, beat for one minute. Repeat with second egg.

Turn mixer to low speed and while it is running, add half of flour mixture, then milk, then remainder of flour. Stop mixer as soon as ingredients are well blended. Add lemon peel and stir.

Spoon batter into pan and bake for 1 hour.

Five minutes before the end of the baking time, combine lemon juice and 6 tablespoons of sugar in a saucepan. Cook and stir over medium heat for a minute or two until the sugar dissolves and the mixture is syrupy.

Pour lemon syrup over the top of the cake as soon as you remove it from the oven. Leave the cake in the baking pan for 15 minutes, then turn onto cake rack to cool completely.

Serves 10

Cheese Cake with Fruit Topping

1½ cups graham cracker crumbs
(about 20 to 24 crackers)
¼ lb. (1 stick) butter or margarine, melted
3 tablespoons sugar
1 teaspoon vanilla
½ pint (1 cup) sour cream

12 oz. cream cheese, softened
¼ lb. farmer cheese
3 eggs, separated
¾ cup sugar
1 teaspoon vanilla
1 can pie filling or 1 cup preserves

The Night Before

Preparation Time: 18 min.   *Cooking Time:* 35 min.

(*Note:* Before starting any preparations, remove cream cheese from refrigerator and let it stand at room temperature to soften.)

Melt butter or margarine and mix with graham cracker crumbs (use blender to make crumbs, or buy a bag of graham cracker crumbs), 3 tablespoons sugar, and 1 teaspoon vanilla. Press crumb mixture into the bottom of an 8-inch spring form cake pan (about 2½ to 3 inches deep). Light oven so that it can preheat to 325°.

Put sour cream, softened cream cheese, farmer cheese, egg yolks, sugar, and vanilla in a large mixing bowl. Beat with an electric mixer or a rotary beater until mixture has a creamy consistency. Beat the three egg whites until stiff, then fold into cheese mixture. Pour this over the crust in the spring form pan. Bake at 325° for 35 min. Then, *without opening the oven,* turn the heat off; leave the cake in the unopened oven for another hour and a half. Then remove from oven, top with pie filling, and refrigerate.

When the cake is cold—either later that night or at any time before serving—remove the sides of the spring form pan.

Serves 8

Banana Pie

baked pie shell, 9 or 10 inches
1 pint sour cream
4 egg yolks, lightly beaten
1 cup sugar
2 tablespoons plus 2 teaspoons
   cornstarch

1½ teaspoons vanilla
2 large or 3 small bananas
3 tablespoons lemon juice
shaved chocolate for garnish

The Night Before

Preparation Time: 12 min.   *Cooking Time: 20 min.*

Bake pie shell according to instructions on package.

Heat sour cream in top of double boiler until thinned and heated through—do not allow it to get so hot that it curdles.

While sour cream is heating, place egg yolks in large bowl, beat lightly, and add sugar and cornstarch. (This mixture will be lumpy and granular.)

Add heated sour cream to egg yolk mixture in bowl, pouring in a little at a time and stirring well after each addition. Return to top of double boiler and cook for 20 minutes. Remove from heat and stir in vanilla. Chill mixture for 30 minutes.

When you are ready to assemble the pie, slice the bananas and spread them out, in one layer, on a dish. Pour lemon juice evenly over banana slices. Let stand for 2 or 3 minutes, then pour off lemon juice.

Place a layer of sliced bananas on bottom of baked (and cooled) pie shell. Mix remaining bananas with chilled sour cream mixture and spoon into pie shell.

Garnish with shaved chocolate. Cover and refrigerate.

Serves 6 to 8

Butterscotch Sauce

This simple sauce can transform ice cream or ice cream and pound cake into a special dessert with very little effort. It will keep for about a week in the refrigerator.

½ cup light corn syrup
1½ cups light brown sugar
4 tablespoons butter

½ cup milk
1 teaspoon vanilla

The Night Before
Preparation and Cooking Time: 9 min.

Place corn syrup, sugar, and butter in a saucepan and cook over high heat, stirring constantly, until mixture boils rapidly. Remove from heat.

Add milk and vanilla; stir thoroughly to blend. Let cool and refrigerate in a covered container.

Before Serving
Preparation and Cooking Time: 5 min.

Reheat sauce over low heat, stirring constantly, until warm. Do not let it come to a boil.   *About 2 cups*

Biscuit Tortoni

1 cup heavy cream
Scant ⅓ cup confectioner's
   (powdered) sugar

1 egg white
½ cup macaroon crumbs
1 to 1½ teaspoons cream sherry

The Night Before
Preparation Time: 15 min.

Prepare macaroon crumbs (the electric blender does this beautifully—and quickly!). Whip the cream. Fold in sugar, a tablespoonful at a time. Beat egg white until stiff. Using about a third of each at a time, fold the following into the whipped cream: the beaten egg white, ⅓ of the cup macaroon crumbs, and the sherry.

Spoon the mixture into paper muffin cups. Sprinkle the tops with remaining macaroon crumbs. Place in freezer, uncovered, until quite firm, then wrap in plastic bag and return to freezer.

Serves 6

Mocha Almond Cream

¼ cup strong coffee
4 oz. (4 squares) semisweet
    chocolate
1 cup superfine sugar
½ lb. sweet butter, softened

¼ cup cherry or orange liqueur
¼ teaspoon almond extract
1 cup finely crushed almonds
2 cups heavy cream, whipped

The Night Before

Preparation Time: 16 min.

Put coffee and chocolate in top of double boiler and cook until chocolate melts, while you start the other preparations.

Pulverize almonds in electric blender.

Cream sugar and softened butter until well blended. Beat in liqueur and almond extract. Continue beating until sugar is so well dissolved that you can neither see it nor feel it. Beat in the crushed almonds. Then fold in the melted chocolate.

Refrigerate the mixture, so that the chocolate cools slightly, while you whip the cream. Fold in whipped cream. Spoon into individual dessert dishes and refrigerate.   *Serves 8*

Pastry Cream

This is not a dessert in and of itself, but it is a part of three desserts in this book (cream puffs, trifle, and strawberry tart) and is also useful as a filling for standard layer cakes. Pastry cream should be cool before it is used as part of another recipe, so prepare it a few hours in advance of the time you will need it, or even the night before the night before.

4 egg yolks
6 tablespoons sugar
¼ cup flour

1½ cups milk
¾ teaspoon vanilla

Preparation and Cooking Time: 9 min.

Separate eggs and mix yolks, sugar, and flour together in small bowl.

Scald milk. Remove from heat.

Pour a little of the hot milk into the egg yolk mixture and stir briskly. Then place saucepan of milk over very low heat (or over boiling water) and very gradually add egg yolk mixture, stirring constantly with a wire whisk. When the cream is very thick and smooth, remove from heat and stir in vanilla.

Cool thoroughly before using in another recipe or refrigerating, stirring occasionally during cooling period.   *2 cups*

Index